FUMBLING THRU FATHERHOOD

Lost, unsure,
tired, confused
... it's all good.

JARED FIEL

ATJA BOOKS
Greeley, Colorado

Published by ATJA Books.
PO Box 337088
Greeley, CO 80633

ISBN: 0-9752819-0-9

Library of Congress Control Number: 2004103217

The columns on which this book is based originally appeared in The Greeley Tribune and The Fort Morgan Times. To the extent they are reprinted here, they are reprinted with permission.

Printed in the United States of America.

10 09 08 07 06 05 04   1 2 3 4 5

DEDICATION

To my wonderful boys, without whom I would not be a dad and would also have no idea what happens to a sticker after it's shoved up a nose.

And to my incredible wife who also had a great deal to do with me being a dad, and who makes me realize every day how happy, lucky and — usually — wrong, I am most of the time.

ACKNOWLEDGEMENTS

Most of my insights into parenting came from three sources:

My parents who provided me with love, laughter and bowling lessons.

My wife and two sons who provide me with practical experience.

And classic TV Land sitcoms, which provide me real lessons and make me constantly think, "What would Ward Cleaver do?"

CONTENTS

JOINT VENTURES

I HATE IT WHEN
THAT HAPPENS

AIN'T THEY CLEVER

INTRODUCTION

People often talk about maternal instincts. Women apparently have the market on knowing what to do based on generations of women who preceded them. It is the maternal instinct to protect and feed and love a child. We guys have our own Dad instincts. Some use the word "paternal" but that reminds me too much of Pat Boone which makes me think that some guys have a natural instinct to wear loafers and cardigans.

There really isn't a name for the Dad instinct. The reason it is not named is because 99 times out of 100, it is wrong.

Maternal instincts have been forged through generations — from Eve to June Cleaver to Marge Simpson — and give women a strong foundation of proven success to build on.

Guys have no such history of success. Men are generally big doofuses. Our instincts are all about humor. That's why we do stupid things with our kids like playing the, "tossing recently fed child in the air" game or playing hockey in the kitchen.

The only instinct that serves us right is to get together with a woman who has all the answers. If you think your significant other doesn't have all the answers, just ask her. Of course she does.

But those answers are BORING.

They say things like, "No, don't swing from there" or "You'll poke your eye out" or "That's disgusting."

No fun.

That's why we are here, guys.

I have learned this one lesson after six years of raising two boys of my own. Without a dad, a child would never know the exhilaration of going too fast or the thrill of poking your eye out.

I started writing about this phenomenon in a regular newspaper column called Fiel's Files. Over the years, I have heard from both dads and moms about how much they enjoyed reading about another father suffering (OK, it was actually MY mom and dad, but the sentiment was still there).

This book is a collection of those thoughts and ideas. I hope this will assist fathers everywhere in honing their own instincts so we can pass them on to our kids.

I mean somebody has to show them how to belch and blame it on the dog, right?

B.B.
(BEFORE BABY)

WEATHER OR FAMILY CHANNEL?

To find out or not to find out?

That is the question every new parent has to answer.

Folks in my parents' generation had to rely on twigs, mud and the eye of a newt to find out the sex of their child.

But parents today can find out about anything they want about their child before it is born; sex, hair color, future earning potential and whether or not he or she will move out at 18 years of age or sponge off the parents for life.

There are two schools of thought on this subject: First, there are the people who want to find out the sex of the child so they can plan clothes, toys, decorations in the room and whether the child will play in the WNBA or the NBA. Second are the people who don't want to know the sex until birth because they are clinically insane.

Seriously some people want to get that surprise in the delivery room. Personally, I am fairly certain I am going to pass out in the delivery room so I want to know now.

My wife was part of the clinically insane group. She insisted that — like our stone-age parents — we would not find out the sex until it was born. I was of the belief that we should find out everything we could now, because I am pretty sure that the minute the baby is born we won't know a darn thing.

I argued that if we knew the sex we could start calling the baby in her belly a "he" or a "she" instead of "it" which I think seriously warps the tiny mind of the kid and turns him or her into a bizarre performance artist, serial killer or politician.

I also pointed out that since my sister works at a children's clothing store she would be able to clothe our kid pretty well in advance, if she knew what sex to buy for.

Despite my logical arguments, my wife appeared dead-set against finding out.

It's not that I really care one way or the other about what sex our baby is. I mean, if it's a boy, I can teach him to play baseball and football and how to catch slimy critters and show them to his mom.

If it were a girl, well, I would like to have a girl because they tend to be more mature, but the last thing I really need is my child to be more mature than I am.

Eventually I wore my wife down with an endless tirade of "C'mon, pleeeeeeeease." She finally decided that she would either have to divorce me or find out the sex and finding out would mean a lot fewer lawyers, so she went along.

The most common way of finding out the sex of the baby is through the ultrasound. This is an amazing device that uses sound waves (I understand the sound is similar to a number of Seattle grunge bands) that bounce off the baby. These bounces are recorded on a screen to draw a picture of the baby.

That's what they tell you at least.

After looking at the picture on the screen, I am now a firm believer that what I was seeing was a satellite weather image of the Atlantic coastline. The friendly lady running the machine pointed to the image and explained the area I thought was New York was actually my baby's head. The railroad tracks leading to New Jersey were the spine.

I was just interested to see if we could see the Florida peninsula or not.

After awhile, my wife and I had been hypnotized enough to believe that we were really seeing inside her belly and not the Weather Channel.

And then out of the fog we saw it. OK, technically, she had to point it out to us and it still looked a lot less like a peninsula and a lot more like a one-boat dock, but it was there!

We are having a boy. That means for the first time ever there will be two males in our house to vote against my wife. Don't get me wrong. I know that two-to-one still doesn't win when the "one" is my wife, but if we end up having about six or so other sons, I might stand a chance.

My wife is more than a little nervous. She now has a lot more things to worry about. She has to fret over potty-training a human sprinkler, teaching him how to make that "toot" sound with his armpit and learning to admire mud pies for their creative expression.

At least, now she has a few months to prepare (or plan her escape).

GOING BACK TO SCHOOL

Birthing classes are taught by women for a reason.

If men taught these classes, it would only take about ten minutes. Professor Guy would stand in front of the class. He would pass out beers for all the husbands. Then he would direct his only comment to the women: "Say this with me: "DRUGS!!!!""

Fortunately, men do not teach these classes.

For those of you who don't know, birthing classes teach humans — who have been having babies for thousands of years, by the way — how to have a baby while hyperventilating.

The classes take several weeks and include a number of graphic video presentations that they really should have shown to these people in the class before they got pregnant.

Narrator: "As you can see, Mary here has entered the first stage of labor. She is calm. She is using her breathing exercises and this contraction hardly seems to phase her."

(Close up on a woman with beads of sweat running down her face. A vein in her forehead looks ready to explode)

B.B. (BEFORE BABY)

Mary: "Ohhhhh this hurts!!! I hate all men! I'm going to kill my husband!! Give me a @#$% EPIDURAL!!!"

These classes also include detailed discussions of all the things that could possibly go wrong. I understand that the reason for this is so that if something goes wrong with your baby, you can handle it. But this also gives those first time parents an image for their nightmares for the next few months.

"If your baby is born with his or her lips on top of his or her head, that is perfectly normal. It will make feeding a little more interesting. But it is all perfectly normal."

These classes also go into all the different positions in which a woman can have a baby. If this were left up to the men, there would be two positions: knocked out and unconscious.

But these classes show how a woman can deliver a baby while squatting, while lying on her side, while hanging from a chandelier or while doing a fancy two-step to "Honky Tonk Moon."

Husbands and wives take these classes together. The ploy the teacher tries to pass off is that the husband is a "coach" in the birthing process. The husband's job is to encourage, support and be something for the wife to grab onto when the pain of a contraction hits.

The truth is the only reason men go to these classes is so the women know where their husbands are and that they are not making a mess in the house.

For the most part, the birthing class is like going back to high school — including the heavy breathing.

Some of the guys in the class are serious students who learn every aspect of the birthing process, know every single breathing style and when the moment of truth arrives, will help their wives deliver a 14-pound kid without any pain and cook an eight-course meal the day the wife comes home from the hospital.

Then there are the guys like me. It's not that we are not supportive, but when put in a classroom setting, we revert back to our immature high school selves.

"Heh, heh, she said `breast.'" And then the guys cheer for the sperm in the "This is How You Got Here" video.

If a guy taught this class, he would say things like, "Now when the water thingy breaks, put on your waders, 'cuz you're going swimmin', dude."

One of the highlights of the class is a tour of the "Family Birth Center" at the local hospital. This is an exciting adventure because instead of being told about all the bizarre tools and monitors, you actually get to see them.

There is one type of monitor that screws into the top of the baby's scalp while he or she is still inside the woman. These are the same people who tell you that a mom drinking caffeine will mess up a child and they are screwing wires into babies!!

The key part of any birthing room — for a guy, at least — is the television. When we walked into the room, the women looked at the bed and the other surroundings. The guys looked for the remote control.

Since my wife and I are having a boy, I can almost guarantee that my son — who will have baseball in his blood — will be born during the World Series. This is going to be the ultimate test of me as a husband and father.

My wife has already made it more than clear that the TV is not to be turned on. So, I asked one of the nurses if they would be willing to bring in updated scores for expectant fathers.

She said once a father told his wife, "OK honey, we got three hours to get this baby out before kickoff."

I thought that sounded cool. My wife didn't.

Apparently I am going to get an F in this class.

PARENT-NOIA
RUNS RAMPANT

Normal.

I have to admit that most of my life I have been against being normal. I don't like popular music. Most of the best-selling movies stink. And there is not one person on the annual list of most intriguing people that interests me at all.

But, now I am going to be a parent and the word "normal" has a completely new meaning.

I used to think it was a cop-out when I would ask a prospective parent if they wanted a boy or a girl and the response would always be: "I don't really care. I just hope it's normal and healthy."

Now that I am on the receiving end of that question, I feel the same way.

I don't wish for superior intelligence or x-ray vision, I just want him to be normal. Like all parents, I fear that my son won't have five fingers or five toes or will have three arms or whatever.

Those nine months seem like the longest of all time when you have those things to be worried about. The doctors explain to you that most kids are born without any problems, but that does nothing to cure the worried mind.

To try to calm down these parents, medical folks have invented all these different types of tests to make sure all the kid's chromosomes and other long words are normal.

My wife and I decided we should take only the most basic test — a blood test to check for a few problems.

Before the test, we were told that because of my wife's age, there was a 220 to 1 chance that our baby would have some type of problem. If someone had told us that we had a 220 to 1 chance of being hit by a car while crossing the street, we'd feel pretty safe.

But adult odds and baby odds are totally different. If cops catch only one speeder out of 100, we feel pretty safe putting the old pedal down. But if one out of 100 babies is hurt because of some newfangled toy, there is no way our kid is going near it.

Needless to say, we didn't feel all that confident with 220 to 1 odds. We wanted more specific information. It's not that we'd feel any less paranoid if the odds were 2 trillion to 1, but at least we were doing something about it.

We took the test and the results came back:

10 to 1.

All of the sudden, our paranoid fears were reality. Our hopes of having a normal child were gone. It was amazing how the thought of our child not being normal hit me. I was breathless and frozen.

Neither my wife nor I realized how much we already loved that lump in her belly until that moment. We held each other — silently praying for those numbers to change.

Ten percent. That may seem like a pretty low figure, but it sounded almost insurmountable to us.

Through my job as a newspaper reporter, I have met a lot of parents of kids who aren't "normal." I thought about my wife and I joining their ranks and I was terrified. Those people all had an inner strength — fortitude — that I was not sure I had.

They had patience and understanding. Before this incident, my biggest fear was toilet training. I didn't have any concept of caring for a kid that was anything other than normal. It was incomprehensible to me.

Our doctor tried to tell us that we still had a 90 percent chance of a normal child. We were focused on the other 10 percent.

Because of that fear of not knowing for sure, our doctor set up another test for two days later. Forty-eight hours.

Both nights were sleepless. My wife and I tried to keep our days busy to keep our minds from wandering back to that 10 percent, but it didn't work.

Finally, the day came. The test we needed required an ultrasound first and the ultrasound technician could tell we were tense.

She put the wand up to my wife's belly and the image of our baby filled the screen. The first thing the technician said was, "This baby's not as old as you think it is." Apparently our original due date was 30 days too early.

We didn't find out for a few tense moments later what that meant. Apparently the odds of a problem in the test are figured based on the due date. Our doctor quickly refigured the results and we found out the odds of a problem were 437 to 1.

The relief on our faces was obvious as the ultrasound technician said, "That's just the first of a million scares you'll have. Welcome to parenthood."

PLAYING THE WAITING GAME

I used to measure time in days, months, years, etc.

When I found out that my wife was pregnant, I started to think about everything in terms of trimesters. (i.e. "The baseball season is about two trimesters long.")

But now — as time has practically come to a screaming halt while we wait for the day our son is going to be born — I only think about seconds, minutes and hours.

I finally realize what the phrase "time is relative" means. It means it seems to take forever for your next relative to be born.

Whenever anyone else I ever knew was pregnant, it always seemed that the pregnancy went by pretty darn quick.

Now I know that by the time I was sure enough they were pregnant to ask them about it, they were probably only a week or so from being in labor.

This is because one of a guy's biggest fears is asking a woman when her baby is due only to be verbally assaulted when the guy finds out she just filled up at an all-you-can-eat bar.

B.B. (BEFORE BABY)

But I have known about my wife's pregnancy for quite a while now, and personally I think it's taking way too long to come to the grand finale.

The first two trimesters of my wife's pregnancy flew by. This is probably because during most of that time my wife was asleep. She was lucky that this was her only pregnancy symptom, but it was pretty serious.

You see, we are not talking about normal sleep. This was hibernation. And I don't care what women say, we men do have sympathy symptoms of pregnancy as well. During this time I slept almost as much as she did.

When I told co-workers that I was suffering from sympathy tiredness, I didn't get any pity or understanding. I may have to start my own support group for this so all of us future fathers can get some guilt-free sleep.

People think that the father's role in pregnancy ends pretty early on, but that's not true. We are the ones who pay for the hash browns and cake ordered at midnight. We are the ones who are forced to speak to our wife's stomach so the baby will know us at least a little. So the time spent during pregnancy is difficult for both parents. Fortunately, we men can still drink beer, so I guess we have a slight advantage.

Anyway, time has now stopped.

It seems like we have been about a month away from this birth for a long time and it certainly doesn't seem like it's getting any closer.

I guess, by nature, I am not a patient person. My wife says I stare at her like a Christmas present that I want to open on Thanksgiving.

I also realize that these long nine months are much harder on my wife, but at least she can feel the little nipper kicking around every so often. I get nothing.

Some friends of ours are due about four weeks before us and they are reaching the end of their patience. In fact, just about every woman I have ever seen who starts measuring the time before the due date in hours gets that same look in her eye that says, "I am so tired of being an incubator. This thing better come out SOON!"

These friends have tried everything to bring this labor about a little sooner. She has eaten spicy foods, watched scary movies and is threatening to take up aerobics.

By far, the worst part of waiting for the baby to come is dealing with the other people.

First there are the people who have had children — and it could have happened last week or 100 years ago, because their response is always the same: advice and horror stories.

"Oh I was 14 weeks overdue and my baby weighed 50 or so pounds, but you'll do fine."

"It may seem like a long time now, but after that baby is born you won't even remember how long it was."

"I was in labor for two weeks and I never took any drugs."

Then there are the people who have never had a child before or just forget how painfully long the process appears to be.

"Isn't that baby here, YET?"

"When's the due date? ... That far off? I thought you would have had it by now."

"Looks like she's ready to pop."

Just as a note of clarification, none of these comments help the time go by any faster.

In fact, I think the only thing that could help is to sleep, but neither one of us are doing any of that now thanks to our son who appears to be practicing in my wife's belly to be the first male Rockette.

For the record, our little dancer will be kicking out at the end of October, or 12,960 minutes and counting ...

NEW PARENTS MAKE EASY TARGETS

Expecting parents are the most susceptible people in the world.

If a soon-to-be parent reads an advertisement that says this product — usually something like a black and white rattle — will increase their child's I.Q., his social skills and his money-generating ability as an adult, that item is as good as sold.

Parents are ruled by guilt. This is an odd concept for me because all I can remember about growing up was feeling guilty for making my mom crazy, but maybe that was her way of sharing the job.

Parents want the best for their kids. And since the parent has no real concept of what the "best" means, we have to rely on so-called experts.

These are people who have studied baby things their entire lives and know what babies need and what will help them develop into normal human beings. Or they are people who get paid gobs of money to lie. It's hard to tell them apart.

For instance, once upon a time someone did a study that demonstrated that infants can only see black and white for the first few months of life and that high-contrast toys would help the child's brain develop faster.

Even now — after thousands of parents painted black and white squares all over nursery walls only to find out that their child still drools and poops like a normal kid — there are still a whole line of black and white toy products out there.

A parent walking into a baby store has an overwhelming experience. But what is worse is getting catalogs at home, where you cannot avoid people trying to sell ergonomically designed high chairs and brand name sunglasses for your child.

We received one catalog that sells rattles. There is even a rattle shaped like a cell phone. I guess it would be cute to see a baby playing with an "adult" item, but what happens when junior gets hold of your real cell phone and dials Hong Kong?

When I was a kid, the only toy I can even remember was one of those jumper seats that hangs off of a doorjamb. You sit the kid in the seat and then he can bounce for hours.

Well, apparently those are no longer considered safe. They still sell them, but if you buy one, the clerk will look at you funny and put you on a list of bad parents that they then turn over to the police.

I thought that one of the simplest purchases we would make for our baby would be the mobile for the crib. All it consists of is a music box and some cute things that spin around above the kid's head when he is lying in the crib.

But, no! It's not so simple. Apparently the mobiles have changed. People finally realized that from the kid's perspective, the only view he had of the fuzzy bears spinning above him was of the bears' crotches. Now, mobiles are tilted so kids can see the whole bear.

No scientist has determined what happened to the thousands of kids who grew up staring at bear crotches, but my guess is that they would not be fun to talk to at parties.

Besides the stuff directed at the kids these catalogs also feature stuff directed at the parents.

For instance, sure, those audio baby monitors are fine for normal parents, but if you want to have a perfectly safe child, you need a video monitor. This gives the parents the ability to watch every single move their child makes to see if they have the potential for a career in music videos.

And then, of course, is the diaper pail. Now they offer these canisters where you put the soiled diaper in and twist the lid, and the diaper is preserved in plastic so thousands of years from now archeologists will be able to tell what your child had for lunch.

The only downside of all these products aimed at new parents is that most new parents are so poor they can't waste a lot of money on this stuff.

Which is where the grandparents come in.

Parents are only one of the most susceptible groups of consumers. Do you know who holds the number one ranking? Yes, you guessed it: expecting grandparents.

My mom told me that she got a catalog for grandparents the other day.

She doesn't know how she got on the mailing list. She doesn't realize that the baby industry knows everything about expecting and new parents, including where the grandparents live.

So, yes, we are already making room for the talking rattles, the bells and whistles playpen (now called a play yard) and the potty seat shaped like a goose.

But I have no idea where my cell phone is.

BUNDLE OF JOY
(AND POOP)

BEING CUTE ONLY JOB BABY CAN DO

Babies are cute.

That's it.

They don't do anything else. That is their job: to look cute.

Oh sure, they cry and they sleep, but the most important thing they do is to be adorable. Other than that, they don't do a darn thing.

Don't get me wrong, I am not bored with my child already, but he just doesn't do ANYTHING!!

My son was born three weeks ago. The day he was born — after the nurses cleaned him up — I held him in my arms while my wife took a well-deserved nap.

I stared at this little human and he stared at me. We appraised each other for a good 30 minutes.

I looked in his eyes and thought about all the baseball games I will take him to, all the fun we'll have together and how much money he is going to cost me as he grows up.

He discovered that I am a large, furry-faced person who does not have anything to feed him and so he went to sleep.

And as I watched my first-born son sleep in my arms, I thought, "OK, now what?"

I will admit that for a moment I considered waking him up just so he might do something — anything. But I restrained myself and held him until my arm went numb.

Since that time, my son and I have spent quite a lot of time together. He stares. I stare. He cries. I hand him off to mom. It's not much of a relationship, but it seems to work for us.

Of course I love my son. But, boy am I ready for him to be able to do something. Currently the only thing I can praise him for is sleeping and not spitting up on me. About once a day, he will raise his head up — this is a major moment since the rest of the time he just sits there.

And don't get me wrong — just sitting there is fine as long as you are watching television or something, but he just sits there. At his age television is something he can interrupt by crying. He can't even tell the difference between Maryann and Ginger.

When I talk to experienced parents about their children, some say this is their favorite time — before they can walk away or talk back. This is the time before your child can run into heavy traffic chasing a ball or tell you to shovel the snow yourself.

As I look back at my own childhood, the most trouble I ever got into happened after I learned to walk and talk. In fact the only time I got in trouble that did not involve me being in the wrong place or saying the wrong thing was when I did NOT do something like taking out the garbage, cleaning up my room or scraping the peanut butter off the ceiling.

But a kid never gets in as much trouble for not doing something good as for doing something bad.

Maybe babies have the right idea. By shutting up and not moving around, they avoid a lot of problems.

Now babies can also be frustrating. They cry. They poop. They cry some more.

That's where the cute-thing comes into play. After three nights of no sleep and the kid starts crying again, it is impossible to get mad at him because he's so darn cute.

And don't tell me that babies don't know they are cute. They know to really turn on the charm after they have just messed up a diaper you spent the last 10 minutes changing.

In theory adults could learn something from babies. If there were a politician who didn't speak, he would never lose an election. If your boss wanted you to run an errand and you couldn't walk yet, you'd be free and clear.

But in the real world, adults just are not cute enough to get away with doing nothing (except, of course, your average supermodel).

Personally, I am ready for my kid to be a little less cute and a little more active. I don't expect him to start playing catch with me in the backyard anytime soon but I am ready for the day when he does more than your average paperweight.

Although he is a pretty cute paperweight.

OUTING THE PARENTS

When I first found out that my wife and I were going to have a baby, I vowed that we would not become "those parents."

Everyone knows "those parents." They are the ones who bring a screaming baby into a crowded restaurant, store or other public place and promptly ruin the day of everyone in a one-block radius who can hear nothing but "WAAaaaaAAAAaaa" for several hours straight.

"Those parents" can be found on airplanes, at concerts, movie theaters and anywhere else where a screaming kid can destroy a peaceful moment.

"Those parents" get looks from other people and others talk about them in whispered tones, "Why would they bring a baby here?" or "What are they thinking?"

I promised myself we would never be that way. I figured parents of newborns should be like lepers and never venture into public until the kid was old enough to muzzle.

Now, our child is nearly eight weeks old and I finally realized why parents take their child out: they are bored. Strangely, the desire to get out of the house not only doesn't go away with a baby, it actually increases.

The only thing that works in the house to quiet him (and then only sometimes) is this activity center he has. He lays on his back on a blanket and looks up at two arching bars hanging full of brightly colored toys and he gets hypnotized.

After days and days of trying to quiet our son in our house, we were ready to get out.

Most of the time, he has been very peaceful on quick shopping trips and other errands because he falls asleep in the car (a trick used by generations of parents).

So we started getting cocky. We decided to take him to the mall while we went Christmas shopping.

We loaded up all the necessary items (as well as two other bags of stuff we knew we wouldn't need but had to have anyway) and went to the mall. Our son was asleep peacefully until we put him in his stroller.

His eyes went wide and we were sure he was going to start wailing. But then his eyes glazed over in his standard hypnotized look.

That was when I noticed that he was looking at all the brightly colored decorations hanging from the ceiling of the mall. Yes, a mall is just an adult activity center!

For the most part he was pretty good. But like any shopper, he started to complain after about an hour.

In our attempt to avoid being "those parents" my wife and I had already scoped out and practiced our emergency crying escape plan. She would pop the pacifier in his mouth as I found the nearest exit. Then we would race there before his screams reached ear-piercing decibels.

Fortunately, we were able to escape with only a few nasty glares from other people. At this point, we figured we had this parent-outing thing down, so we pushed our luck.

We decided to go out to a restaurant for dinner.

We made sure he had plenty to eat so he would sleep through our meal. We found a table in the back of the restaurant within running range of the restroom (which is where all parents take crying babies because it amplifies the sound as it echoes in the enclosed space).

We whispered our order to the waitress so we wouldn't wake him up and we cringed as the minutes went on until our meal was at the table — sure that he would wake up and start wailing.

But he was quiet. Only as I brought the final bite of my dinner to my mouth did he start to make noise. We were able to grab him, pay the bill and run out the door before he hit full bore.

My wife and I just assumed we had the perfect baby. We could take him anywhere and he would be great.

We didn't even think much about it when we decided to go to a Christmas band concert last week with him.

He was fed. He was warm. We got seats on the aisle just in case we had to make a mad rush for the door. And he was sleeping.

Then the music started. The drums. The brass. The singing. I was sure my son would try to join the chorus with his own version of "I'm Dreaming of a Whining Christmas" at top decibel. But he still slept.

My wife and I relaxed. We avoided being "those parents" again.

Then, as the first song ended, the packed house applauded ... LOUDLY. His eyes flew open, his arms flung out and he screamed in top form.

We were caught off guard and were not very quick about gathering our coats and various baby luggage and heading for the exit.

As the applause died down, his screaming continued. We got "the looks" and I noticed quite a few people whispering.

So I'd like to say to all "those parents" out there that we are proud to be part of the club.

GRANDMAS ARE MOMS-LITE

When I was growing up, my mom was the enemy.

My sister and I plotted schemes and concocted lies that only kids could tell in a concerted effort to drive our mom nuts.

My dad was Switzerland. He didn't want to get involved in any of it. I am pretty sure that he was silently rooting for my sister and me, but when backed into a corner he would always turn into the enforcer for mom.

Since it was basically us against my mom and she could not watch everything we did, she would try to rule by remote control. This would involve her yelling at us from three rooms away to make sure we were not shaving the dog or doing anything else that would send her to the funny farm.

"What are you kids up to?" she bellowed.

"Noooothing," we sang in the sweet unison of children who were really doing something pretty awful.

"Are you playing with matches?" she screeched.

"NOooooo," we said in the tone that all kids use to lie with. In fact, I am pretty sure that it would pass a lie detector test because when kids say "NOooooo" they know it means yes.

"Are you doing anything that involves any harmful chemicals?"

She continued through on her laundry list of things we could be doing: "Could what you are doing be fatal?" "Will it require professionals to clean-up?" and "Will the SPCA need to be contacted?"

Every question got the same answer: "NOooooo." This continued until mom got so fed up she got up to see what we were doing.

Fortunately for us, this usually took long enough for my sister and me to run away from the scene of the crime.

That was then. Now mom is grandma, and it's amazing how she is no longer the enemy. In fact, she has become an ally.

She came to visit last week. Before our son was born, my wife and I would entertain my parents by taking them out to movies or some other local hot spot. Now, my mom comes alone (apparently bringing my father would only cut down on the amount of time my mom can hold our son) and she baby-sits so my wife and I can go out and have fun. ("Having fun" as defined by parents means going shopping for more baby junk.)

Grandma likes to get us out of the house because she can do all the things with our son that my wife (who, strangely enough, is now the mom) won't allow because she is afraid he will get hurt.

As dad, I have to try to be Switzerland, but it is really hard.

When we came home from shopping, my wife started cleaning up the house while grandma, my son and I went into a back bedroom to look at his new toys.

We tore open the packages and started playing with the stuff. Grandma laughed. My son giggled. I was just trying to be Swiss, but I cracked and shoved a colorful rattle into my son's mouth.

38

"You are not opening those toys and letting our son put them in his mouth before they can be washed, are you?" the new mom yelled from the kitchen.

We all stopped laughing. My son knew we were in trouble and he looked back and forth between grandma and dad.

I looked into my mom's eyes and I saw the fun, carefree spirit that I never saw when she was just my mom. Not having to worry all the time will do that for you, I guess.

We locked eyes for a short moment as we considered my wife's long-distance query, and then, in unison, we sang out, "NOooooo."

WHEN DO I START SLEEPING THROUGH THE NIGHT?

I never knew why there was such a thing as 3:30 a.m. until I became a parent.

B.B. (Before Baby) my wife and I never did anything at 3:30 a.m. In fact most 3:30 a.m.s passed us by and we never really missed them.

But now we have become intimate friends with 3:30 a.m. This is the time my son thinks is 7 a.m. — time to wake up and greet the world. After only a few nights of hearing a horrible screeching scream from our child at this time, we knew it was time to get up.

So 3:30 a.m. has become a part of our family schedule — we know this is the time we will be jolted from a peaceful slumber, never to see it again until the next night.

And then last week we got a surprise.

At promptly 3:30 a.m., I woke up. Apparently, my body did not think it could take too many more heart-stopping screams snagging my mind away from dreamland, so I woke up in anticipation.

I curled myself into a ball as I awaited the impending sonic blast that my son reserves for just such an occasion.

But there was nothing.

The clock got to 3:32 a.m. and I started to worry.

I tried to do that super-human hearing trick everyone has tried when they want to hear a sound in a perfectly quiet house. Still nothing.

I had to get up, if I really wanted to investigate. But it was a little chilly, so I waited a few more minutes for signs of my child's shrill scream. Still nothing.

Finally I got up and checked on him. I poked my head under the canopy of his cradle with a little trepidation. I guess I was expecting him to try a new trick and wait until I least expected it before he let loose with his acoustical assault on my ears.

But it never came. All I heard were the wonderful rhythmic sounds of his breathing. It brought back memories of all those times when I used to make those wonderful sleeping sounds at 3:30 a.m.

Secure in the knowledge that my son was perfectly safe as well as the fact that I was sure he would be waking and screaming any minute, I returned to bed to enjoy those final moments under some toasty covers.

As I slipped back into bed, my wife woke up — startled.

"Oh no, is he OK?"

"He's fine. He's sleeping."

"What? Doesn't he know it's 3:30 a.m.?" my wife asked because — as I said before — life in our house is just a bit messed up.

"Yes, apparently he does. And he is sleeping. Go back to sleep," I said.

We both rolled over and pretended to nod off. But we were both thinking the same thing: Something must be wrong.

Well, technically, my wife was probably thinking that I had not accurately assessed my son's condition and she would wait until I fell back asleep so she could check on him herself without offending me.

Either way, neither one of us slept. We just lay there and waited for him to wake up screaming. One hour. Two hours. Three hours and it was finally time for us to wake up.

And our son screamed! It was a glorious sound. It meant two things: our son was OK, and he had finally slept through the night for the first time.

My wife and I were so happy — and so tired.

I made sure I told everyone at work. And they all said, "Oh, it must feel so good to finally get some sleep."

My wife and I are still waiting for the sleep part. We still wake up a little nervous around 3:30 a.m. This is obviously part of a parent's evolution because when I was in high school and I came home late, my parents always woke up at that exact same moment.

So we're done with one worry, but we have plenty more to go.

ANOTHER SPUD ON THE COUCH

Football is fun.

Hockey is okay.

Don't even get me started on basketball. (I don't really consider it a sport, but we can talk about that some other time.)

Baseball is the best.

I have been impatiently waiting for opening day since the closing game of the last World Series.

My wife, on the other hand, enjoys the off-season because then I am available to help out with stuff around the house. She knows that once baseball season starts, I become completely useless.

There is something about the bright, hot sun and the smell of the grass and the speed of the throws and the snap of the mitt that makes me want to enjoy it all on TV in my dark, cool basement, drinking a beer and not moving a muscle for three hours.

My wife and I have a standing agreement that she can force me to do just about anything (holding her purse while she is trying on clothes, buying feminine products for her at the grocery store, etc.) for her during the off season if she leaves me alone when baseball games are on.

This has worked pretty well for almost four years. But now we have a kid and the rules have changed.

Like any dad, I had images of my son and me sitting down to watch baseball together. He would ask me about a rule or a certain player, and, like my dad did with me, I would fake an answer.

We would play catch after the game, and I'd show him how to scratch himself without getting really obscene.

Then I realized my son is barely six months old. He doesn't even understand the concept of patty-cake. What chance do I have of pretending to tell him the difference between a curve ball and a slider?

Although he is a little young, he is pretty smart. And he has half of my genes in him, so he should enjoy baseball. (Of course, he has half of my wife's genes in him, too, so he could end up becoming a major fan of ice-skating and tap dancing.)

I figured I had a 50-50 shot at making my son a baseball fan, even at this young age. After all, they tell you to read to kids when they are this young even though all they want to do is drool on the pages.

So my son and I sat down to watch the opening day game. He sat on my lap and was immediately entranced by the TV screen. That got my hopes up because I recognized his blank stare as the same one I get when I'm watching the game.

Throughout the first half inning, he just stared. He occasionally giggled. I made myself believe that he was happy that my team — The Colorado Rockies — was doing well.

But then there was a third out and the commercials came on. And my son sat in my arms and laughed. It was one of those really annoying commercials where a local car dealer comes on wearing a Rockies' uniform and talks about hitting home run sales.

My son loved it.

It was followed by another stupid commercial at which my son giggled even more.

I surfed around a little and noticed that my son smiled at just about everything on the screen — including CNN, TNN and even the Weather Channel.

I suddenly came to the conclusion that my son does have my genes. Sadly, they aren't the baseball genes. They are the genes that allow me to sit in front of a television for hours watching completely inane programs and never noticing how bad the programming is.

Yes, my son is a born couch potato.

THAT NASTY, TWO-LETTER WORD

For the first nine months of my son's life, I didn't have to say no to him.

Whenever I see a parent in a store with a child it always seems like "no" is the only word the parent is able to say.

"Mommy, can I ...?"

"No."

"Daddy, I want a ..."

"No."

Even with only a one-word vocabulary, parents are able to communicate a lot of meaning with that one word by using different tones and inflections.

There's the "no" that means, "I don't think that would be a good idea, but I might change my mind later." This is usually followed by the "no" that means, "Now you are bugging me so let's drop the subject." Which is followed by the "no" said through clenched teeth that says, "One more word and you are getting socks for Christmas."

I realized these days were ahead of me, but I wanted to keep them away as long as possible. That day has come.

For the first nine months, my son was unable to do anything that was dangerous enough to demand the use of the word, "no". Since he couldn't move anywhere, my wife and

I just never put him near anything we didn't want him to play with.

And if, by sheer determination and a pretty good use of his butt-wiggle muscles, he was able to get within arm's reach of something bad, all we had to do was pick him up and move him back to safety.

But now he is crawling — and I mean, crawling quickly.

My wife and I were so proud as he took his first few awkward steps. I had my arm around her and we smiled as we watched our son scoot across the floor.

The moment turned from sentimental to terrifying when we saw that he was headed toward the 8-foot-high bookshelves that house enough hardback novels to bury our son and still have enough left over to keep a librarian busy for several weeks.

Fortunately we stopped him before he hurt himself, but that has now turned into our job. As parents, we used to have the jobs of feeder, warm place to sleep and play toy but now all those are secondary to our roles as super heroes who snatch our son from the jaws of death (or at least a bad bruise) only to set him in another direction where he could hurt himself in a new way.

This happens, of course, because kids do not go where you want them to go — ever.

Parent: "Looky, here's a brand new toy that has lots of fun stuff for you to do."

Baby, thinking: "Naw, I think I'll go over to play with the bag of broken glass at the top of the stairs while sticking my finger in an electrical outlet."

Everyone knows about Murphy's Law, but few realized he had children and they made their own law, "Anything that your kids can do wrong, they will do wrong."

All of this new mobility wouldn't be so tough if I had not broken my ankle a few weeks ago. My wife now has to deal with two people crawling all over the house and my son is quicker than I am which makes life a little more exciting.

Of course, now we are doing all the baby-proofing things that we were told to do months ago in all of our parenting books. This means putting covers over outlets, gates at the top of the stairs and removing every piece of furniture in the house because of its potential to hurt an infant.

Even with all that done, my son manages to find new ways to put himself in peril. And since I can't catch up to him, all I can do is say, "no" in my most stern, fatherly voice.

Unfortunately, he hasn't the foggiest idea what the word means and has now interpreted it to mean, "Daddy can't stop you from doing that, so go ahead and try it."

So when my wife asks if I will watch the baby for awhile, I tell her "no". After all, she's the only other person in our house who knows the true meaning of the word.

ROAD ROOKIES

It was not what you might call military precision.

We didn't mean to undertake such a major operation, but it became unavoidable. Our goal was fairly simple: go to my wife's mom's house (a one-hour drive) for Thanksgiving.

It seemed simple. We have done it many times before. But we forgot a major stumbling block to any such plan ... we have a baby now.

This fact means a total shift in thinking and strategizing about how to achieve our goal.

If it was just my wife and I, we would get dressed, I'd wait around for her to be ready and then we would leave.

A baby adds at least two days of planning and a trunk-full of items to the process.

First, we have to pack all the items for the baby. This means diapers, wipes, pacifier, clothes, and more clothes for after he spits up on the others, toys (for dad), blankets, Social Security card, application for college, etc.

My wife planned to stay over for the weekend so this required another few hours of packing to get her stuff together.

At this point we had two suitcases, three bags, and a crying baby. The baby was crying because he needed to eat.

Apparently anytime you want to go anywhere, your baby is hungry.

So, then he ate. Our car nearly buckled under the strain of the items stuffed inside, but we finally got the baby in the car with all of the other items we needed to bring.

My wife then decided she had to ride in the backseat so she could watch the baby. This is not a new thing for us. It is actually a relief to have her looking at our baby rather than my driving for a change. I have grown used to being the chauffeur for my wife and son.

This is the first sign of rookie parents.

In fact if you ever see a couple approaching in a car where the man is driving and the woman is riding in the back looking into a car seat, you had better run unless you want to be stuck looking at hours of baby photos and hearing stories about the adorable "coo" he uttered the night before.

Rookie parents are a dangerous breed. I believe it may stem from the lack of sleep, but they cannot resist telling everyone they know (and hundreds of people they don't) about every minor aspect of how their child is the most beautiful, most talented and smartest kid of all time.

Anyway, we were on the road looking like the Beverly Hillbillies (if they had a chauffeur).

Of course, everyone else on the road was on their way to Thanksgiving somewhere else, too. And most of these folks — I noticed — were veteran parents.

Veteran parents are equally easy to spot. They are usually driving a minivan of some sort with the kids sitting in the backseats (they are apparently kept submissive by mental telepathy from the parents), mom is in the passenger seat telling dad that he is driving wrong and all they need to bring is mom's purse and some fabulous dessert that mom apparently had plenty of time to prepare.

A veteran mom's purse is an amazing thing. There is nothing that a kid needs that can't be found inside. She can produce Band-Aids, chewing gum, gauze, toys, diapers, and nail clippers all from the same purse and still have room left for Lifesavers and quarters for video games.

At least this is the perception of us rookie parents.

We pulled up to a stoplight next to the veteran parent poster family. The mom looked over at our packed car, my wife in the backseat and my son crying like he was being tortured and she nearly laughed.

Eventually my son quieted down and fell asleep. My wife just stared at him.

Now, I should have realized that a rookie mom that does not have a crying baby to worry about would invent something to worry about.

"He shouldn't be sleeping this long," she said. "Do you think something is wrong?"

"No Dear."

"Have you noticed these marks on his face? It looks like acne. But it's only on that one cheek. That's where I normally kiss him. Do you think he could be reacting badly to my Chapstick?"

"No Dear."

"He's breathing funny again. Do you think that's a problem?"

"No Dear."

This continued on for the entire trip. We unloaded our bounty into my mother-in-law's house and she looked at us with that same veteran mom's look that says simply: "Rookie."

DINING GUIDE

TAKE A BITE OUT
OF KIDDIE CRIME

I wanted my son to grow up to be whatever he wanted to become.

I just never thought he would become lunch.

My son's big break came a few weeks ago. I found out about it when my wife called me at work sounding upset.

In the few months that my wife and I have been parents, I have discovered that my wife has many different degrees of being upset. The level I heard on the phone that day was somewhere between "Our son's ear has fallen off" and "Our son spit up all over the carpet."

In other words, I knew it wasn't terribly serious.

"Another kid bit our son," she said to me as if he was now damaged goods for the rest of his natural life.

I told her to take a few deep breaths and to tell me what happened. She said that he had been sitting innocently in day care when another kid — an older infant and a "known repeat biter" (that's one of those things that will wind up on his permanent record and keep him from going to a good college when he grows up) walked up to our son and chomped on his cheek.

My son was defenseless. No teeth. Not able to walk away. So he used his only weapon — a glass-shattering scream — to scare this Hannibal Lecter, Jr. away.

The dining experience had left a dark red mark on our son's cheek, but it did not break the skin.

Then I uttered the first of what I'm sure will be many more phrases that I learned from my father: "Ah, it'll toughen him up."

I think most fathers have developed this "whatever doesn't kill them, toughens them up" philosophy as a defense mechanism for dealing with our wives who don't want a tough baby and who believe anyone who tries to toughen them up should be killed.

My wife insisted that I come home immediately to witness this horrible mark on our son's beautiful face and to document it. I didn't ask the reason for needing documentation. I guess I assumed she was planning to take this "repeat biter" to court (The case of "Turn the other cheek … I want seconds" next on "Judge Judy").

My son did have a definite mark on his cheek, but he certainly didn't seem hurt. In fact, when I came in the door he was enjoying his favorite pastime: watching the ceiling fan and smiling.

Seeing that he was OK, I determined that this was a pretty funny incident. "I guess I can't call him MUNCH-kin anymore, huh?" Then, I said, "We should cover him in Tabasco and that kid won't touch him again."

My wife didn't appreciate my humor.

I decided I better call my mom. We should have a direct line to her by now because she insists on knowing everything that is happening with our son.

My mom's response was vengeance: "Well, he should have gummed the @#$% out of that little bugger."

If it is humanly possible, grandmothers, I believe, are more protective than mothers are. In fact, I would not have been surprised if my mom would have jumped in a plane and flown immediately from California to Colorado to hunt down the little cannibal in person.

In the background I heard my dad. He was trying to determine why my mom was upset. She quickly relayed the story, emphasizing the fact that her grandchild was wounded.

And like one of those annoying Memorex commercials, I heard my dad repeat my earlier statement, "Ah, it'll toughen him up."

But it looks like I won't have to worry about my son being an appetizer for another kid for much longer.

My son finally figured out how to defend himself: his first tooth came in this week.

BABY FOOD GROUPS: STRAINED, SLIMY AND STICKY

Kids who don't eat everything put in front of them are called picky eaters.

Now that I know what kinds of foods people put in front of kids, I completely understand a youngster's reluctance.

When I went shopping for my son's first foods, I was pretty excited. My son was about to join the world of culinary delights and I was going to be his tour guide.

As I walked down the baby food aisle, I soon discovered that this was not going to be much of a tour.

To help out parents who are trying to introduce foods to a baby, baby food companies have developed food in stages. For instance, Stage 1 is various strained vegetables minced and watered down. By the time you get to Stage 4 it includes chunks of unidentifiable goop in a sea of concentrated beet juice.

If I were a baby, I'd get through those four stages as quickly as possible so I could finally have a pizza and a Coke.

I assumed these baby food companies must know something about babies (an assumption I later regretted) so

I picked out a few Stage 1 foods such as minced carrots, mashed green peas and pureed bananas.

Although all of these foods were different colors of slop, they all smelled exactly the same — which should have been a warning.

But I continued on and I scooped a little of the carrots onto a baby spoon and put it in my son's mouth. He made a face that reminded me of, well, someone who had just been served lukewarm strained carrot soup.

He reopened his mouth, and like a Pez dispenser, his tongue ejected my edible offering.

This process continued with the bananas and the peas. The only difference was the color stain on the front of his clothes.

Since that experiment failed — or my son was successful, depending on how you look at it — my wife and I decided to try some real (a.k.a. non-jarred) food.

The problem here is that my wife (a life-long vegetarian) and I (a life-long slave to junk food) have two entirely different concepts of "real" foods.

The first thing my wife gave our son was avocado. She sliced up the green, slimy, disgusting, vegetable-fruit and placed it in front of my son.

And he ate it.

He squeezed it in his hands (apparently he liked that feeling) and shoved the paste he created in his mouth — and went back for more. We have now determined that my son will only eat slimy foods. He loves a raw banana (in its pre-strained mode) and just about any fruit or vegetable that makes a horrible mess (both visually and on a sticky-scale) when he eats it.

We thought our son was a picky eater, but really he is just a connoisseur of mess.

Dinnertime is now an event in itself. My wife and I fix our dinners — I make a heaping plate of artery-clogging meat substance and my wife makes a meal she can graze on — and we fix our son up with his slimy supper.

To avoid anyone losing their respective appetites, no one watches anyone else eat in our house.

We scarf down our meals in relative silence, until my son decides he has had enough. I don't think this means that his stomach is full, but rather that there is not one spot on his body that is not covered in food slime.

We know our son is finished when the food hits the floor. He developed this technique over a few weeks, but he now has it down to a science.

He waits until there is a moment when both my wife and I are distracted by our own feeding frenzy. He then raises his goop-laden hand in the air and dangles a large chunk of gummy, green ooze and waits for us to look up.

Just as we shout the words, "No" or "Don't even think about it," he wrinkles his nose in a laugh and drops the food onto the carpet, which was, at one time, brown but now looks like a pack of human-sized green snails have left trails around the entire room.

Then it came to me. Why they call it being picky. Because that's what the parents have to do with it.

ROCKS: NOT JUST FOR BREAKFAST ANYMORE

My wife doesn't know much about boys. She grew up with her sister and her mom and the only thing she learned about boys she learned from her cousins who spent much of their time trying to blow up amphibians with firecrackers.

Now that she is raising a member of the male species, she doesn't quite know what to do.

She expects our son to behave like a little girl — but this kid doesn't want anything to do with that.

My wife wants our son to conform to this vision she has in her mind. It's a vision of a child that doesn't exist in the real world.

In her mind, a child walks on the sidewalk, avoids mud, finds spiders and other bugs repulsive, doesn't make a loud Pfffthhh sound in a quiet room and only puts things in his mouth that were intended to be digested.

She is only now slowly realizing she is not raising a child. She is raising a son.

The first lessons came with the first snow.

My wife wrapped our son in 56 layers of clothes and took him outside to take part in his first experience with the cold white stuff. She fully expected our 16-month-old son to gently bend over, touch the snow with a heavily gloved hand and shiver with the excitement of the new experience.

But of course, my son — as I have stated before — is a boy.

Boys don't experience things by quality — they do it in quantity, volume, and with speed and with no regard for the safety of themselves or others.

When my son saw the front yard covered in snow, he did not see a pristine, peaceful scene of nature's beauty. He saw it as a part of the world that he had not screwed up yet.

He ran into the snow-covered grass, fell down, got up, ran again, fell again and then stayed down so he could figure out what all the white stuff stuck to him was.

With that Norman Rockwell moment gone, my wife waited some time before trying something like that again.

The next time she wanted to share an outdoor experience with our son, the snow was gone. She led him outside again and onto the lawn where she wanted to watch him play gleefully on the green grass.

My son — who is a boy, by the way — ran across that glorious strip of grass and went directly for the dirt and rocks in our planters. He scooped handfuls of mud and squeezed them in his hand. He found a stick and started hitting it against everything he could see.

And then he found the rocks. Rocks reach an ancient part of a man's brain. It is a part of the brain that goes back eons to a time when a good rock was a weapon, tool and, of course, a cool thing to throw.

Throwing rocks is so ingrained in a man's brain that he is unable to resist the urge. If a man was stuck on a desert island with just one rock — a perfect rock that could slice open coconuts, cut trees down for a hut and kill any dang critter he wanted for dinner — he would be unable to resist the urge to throw it into the ocean to see how many time he could make it skip.

My son picked up a rock and threw it. Then he picked it up again, tried to eat it and threw it again.

Eventually he just held onto the rocks. He would occasionally suck on them for comfort. This drove my wife nuts. Her mind was whizzing with all the disgusting microbes and bacteria my son was ingesting. When she tried to take away the rocks, my son screamed.

She told me about the problem. I wasn't much help.

"God made dirt and dirt don't hurt," I said.

She then remembered that I was of the same species as her son and decided not to ask my advice on anything again.

I didn't know how she resolved the situation until the next day. I was unloading the dishwasher and I found several rocks inside which my wife had placed in there to decontaminate them.

I gotta admit. She's learning.

FROM DOUBLE COVERAGE TO MAN-ON-MAN

THE DEUCE

Two. It's a nice round number. It made sense that we'd want to have two children.

My wife and I each have only one other sibling. It made sense that our family would be that size, too.

My Dad came from a family of six. My mom came from a family of three. My mother-in-law came from a family so big they pretty much lost track of the number of siblings. And all of our parents, when it came to deciding how many kids they wanted, said, "I think two is plenty."

So my wife and I had vowed to have two children. We wanted our son to have a sibling to ... well, my wife would say, "love and play with" and I would say, "to torment."

But no matter the reason for wanting two kids, we had pretty much settled on having two.

And now we have Kid Number Two on the way.

Yes, around December, our family will be complete. We will have achieved everything we ever wanted in a family way and we should be happy.

But while two was always a nice, round number, we had never really thought about the fact that two babies are: TWICE AS MANY BABIES AS WE HAVE NOW!

Double.

Everything.

Double the crying. Double the screaming. Double the diapers.

And, you know that wonderful moment in the mornings, before everyone is awake when the world is peaceful, birds sing and you think you are just happy to be alive? Well, all the OTHER time in the world is doubled so these moments don't exist anymore. Get over it!

My wife and I barely made it through the first two years of our firstborn. I have no idea what made me think we could handle it doubled.

Through the miracle of modern medicine, my wife and I were told that the fuzzy picture on the sonogram had that essential piece of fuzz that means we are having another boy.

When I first found that out, I was pretty excited. "Yes, I don't have to pay for any weddings!" I yelled.

The ultrasound technician — who is also a mother of four boys—quickly informed me, "That's the least of your worries."

And that's when it hit me. We are having two boys — two youngsters who will do all the terrible things I did to my parents — in stereo!

My parents were smart enough to have a boy and a girl so the insanity was at least balanced out a little.

But I won't have a little girl who will tell me all the nasty things her big brother did behind my back. I won't have a sweet little angel who will sit quietly while her older brother tears apart the restaurant.

Nope, I get double the fun of one boy. Whenever you get two boys together, it always leads to the inevitable game of "Bet ya can't..." This game is the leading cause of boys under the age of 35 being admitted to the hospital.

If I had a girl, the conversation between siblings would be like this:

Boy: "Bet ya can't jump off the roof, bounce off the cat and land in the wading pool full of Jell-O."

Girl: "You're right. I'm telling Dad."

But I will have two boys who will do this:

Boy #1: "Bet ya can't stick your G.I. Joe all the way up your nose."

Boy #2: "Can too, but don't tell Dad until we have to call 911!"

So, yes, I will be avoiding those dreaded discussions with wedding florists and their ilk, but I'll be spending plenty of time in emergency rooms, principal's offices and hardware stores (to repair the inevitable damage).

Wish me luck.

TWO IS ENOUGH

It was final's week in college. I had three term papers and four final exams waiting for me in those last five days.

In the middle of the week, I had to play 14 straight games of racquetball to make up for the classes I missed during the regular year because my roommates and I had a bet on the Showcase Showdown on "The Price is Right," which happened to come on at the same time as my class.

I had a total of four hours of sleep in five days. I was nearly comatose with exhaustion at the end of the last test.

I thought that was as tired as I could get — ever.

Now, I have two kids and I would pay a large amount of money to feel a tenth as good as I did at the end of that finals week.

Parenthood means being tired. The word comes from the Latin *paren*, meaning "never sleeps," and *thood*, which means "the sound your head would make if you had time to lay it on a pillow."

My wife doesn't seem to understand that the reason she is so tired is directly related to the fact that we have twice as many children as we had last year.

The other day, my wife of nearly six years sent me a fax on which she spelled my name wrong. Now, I know my name is a little odd, but she's been writing it for quite a while now. She is just so tired that only the basic life-sustaining brain cells are clicking.

But on that same day, she actually hinted to me that she wouldn't mind having a third child.

Huh?

I guess that kind of cognitive dissonance is vital to propagating the species. It's probably a defense mechanism that ol' Mama Nature slipped into women so they will continue to want children.

I have heard it in other women, too. I have seen exhausted women say with a straight face, "It was tough going from one to two kids, but going from two to three was easy."

This is a slogan that has sold more than a few triple-wide strollers, I bet.

My wife also doesn't seem to recall the agony of pregnancy. For nine months, all I heard was a combination of her fear that her ankles would explode or that our second son would never be born and would graduate from high school still in utero.

Now when she talks about the pregnancy to other women (grass roots are a major part of Mother Nature's multiple-kid campaign) she says things like, "It wasn't that bad," or "Sometimes I miss being pregnant."

To counterbalance this would-be population explosion the gods created marriages. The male of the species was intended to be the one who would remember the every-30-second potty dashes and the "I can't ever get comfortable" phases.

Therefore I consider it my job — no, my duty — to put my foot down and remind my wife that we only wanted two kids and we will be happy with two kids. No more, no less.

Of course, the gods also gave the male of the species the absolute inability to ever turn down the one thing that would bring about a third child, so I know none of us men really stand a chance.

IT'S HARD TO
BE ORIGINAL

When we were growing up, my sister thought she had found the ultimate loophole to being second-born.

She convinced herself (she was only 6 years old so it didn't take much convincing) that because her birthday was before mine in the year, eventually she would become older.

I tried to show her that, yes, for a brief 43 days, she would be only three years younger than me, but the rest of the year, I was — and always would be — four years older.

I never understood my sister's obsession with wanting to be the oldest.

Until now ...

Both my wife and I are firstborns. And when we had our son, we had a whole house full of firsters. Then along came our second son.

This was a whole new area for us. And after many months of examining his situation, I have come to the conclusion that being born second STINKS.

I never understood why my sister was so upset that her baby book was never completed (OK, so all it contained was her name and the approximate date she was born) while our parents had completed my book with everything from the receipt from my first doctor's visit to a lock of my baby hair.

Now that my youngest son has opened my eyes to the plight of the seconders, I see this bias all around. A guy I used to work with often referred to his second as "No. 2 Son." I'm pretty sure that sort of thing is what sends kids to therapy.

I am going to try to avoid these types of things with my younger (is that the P.C. term?) son, but I know I have already failed.

I remember the moment that my first son stood up for the first time. My wife and I were practically moved to tears as we watched our first-born beam with pride in his accomplishment.

The second time around, my Beta son (too scientific) pulled himself up and we smiled and said, "OK, now walk to Daddy." This kid doesn't stand a chance of impressing us unless he starts doing handstands and singing the opening verse of "Stairway to Heaven" in the next few weeks.

Now that I recognize this problem, you would hope that I could change my ways. I didn't, however, take into account that children are very attuned to fake praise.

When No. 2 (OK, it's easier to say, sorry!) first ate Cheerios by picking them up himself, I played it up like he had just pitched a no-hitter in game seven of the World Series.

"OH YEAH!! THAT was awesome, bud. YOU ARE THE MAN!!!"

My youngest son stared at me like I had just told him Mickey Mouse was a gerbil. He just stared. No smile. No glee.

So now I don't know what to do. I really don't understand how kids who are seventh or eighth on the family tree have any egos at all.

At that point, parents probably watch those first few baby steps and say, "OK fine, call me when you can drive a car."

As I watch my latter child (OK, that one is no good) I can't help but look back through his eyes at my days of growing up with my sister.

She couldn't impress teachers because I had taken the same class from them four years earlier.

She couldn't do anything more stupid than I had already done to rebel against our parents.

She didn't stand a chance. But she was also smart enough to learn from my mistakes — especially on ways to fly under our parent's radar.

My younger son now faces that same uphill battle. This summer, we visited my sister and I noticed she was spending quite a bit of time with No. 2 — probably passing on pointers.

I think ol' No. 1 better look out.

EXCEPTIONS TO THE RULE

Despite what most women think, we men are not complete morons.

Yes ladies, we know what you think of us. The problem is that you simply don't understand us. We are complicated creatures who survive based on a set of unbending and unquestionable "rules."

These rules are things we have learned. (Yes, we are capable of learning.)

They are our guiding principles and beliefs.

It is very difficult for a rule to meet all the criteria we men demand before the rule is accepted and followed. When a woman says, "I told you not to mix reds and whites in the laundry," she doesn't understand that we have not completely accepted this new rule into our consciousness. She just thinks we are stupid.

But there comes a time (According to my wife it must be the 101st time because she always says, "I've told you this a hundred times...") when the rule is accepted, believed, followed and strictly adhered to.

Here are a few that have made it into my mind over the years:

1. Don't drive with your knees.

2. Empty cereal boxes belong in the trash, not back in the cupboard. Apparently this rule also covers milk jugs and empty juice containers, but these matters require further research.

3. Yelling while watching sporting events on television will not affect the outcome of the event — but it always feels really good.

4. Don't throw babies in the air after they have just eaten.

5. Anything that says "fat-free" tastes terrible even if people say things like, "It tastes just like the real thing."

6. Everyone else in the world is a worse driver than I am (even when I'm driving with my knees).

7. Discussions of, and examples of, most human bodily functions are not appropriate while at the family dinner table.

The last rule on this list was added very early on in my relationship with my wife. Throughout months (my wife would say years) of rather embarrassing trial and error, this rule made it into my consciousness and I have religiously lived up to it.

That's what men do. We learn a rule. We live by the rule and things never change.

These rules are the basis for how men have survived and prospered. We don't make exceptions to our rules and our rules help us get through life.

And Rule No. 7 seemed just fine with me. If I really needed to discuss a human bodily function, there were plenty of other times and people to talk about it with. (This is actually a pretty major topic of discussion among men in bars or at sporting events.)

But now I have discovered Rule No. 7 no longer applies. This is because in our house we have recently had to begin "potty training." Actually, my wife and I are pretty good at it. It's our oldest son who needs some work.

And because we are involved in this process, everything we do or say is somehow connected to two of the bodily functions that I know were specifically banned under Rule No. 7.

The rule started to bend when we had our first child and my wife would ask me — in the middle of dinner — to describe in detail the contents of the diaper I had just changed.

Now that we have an infant and a 2-year-old, it seems as though every conversation is about peeing and pooping. We are either talking about doing it or describing it or planning for it or deciding when would the best time to do it or whatever.

And yes, it has even crept into our dinner conversations. Even when we are eating out and run the risk of being overheard by people who don't know about the child-exemption from Rule No. 7.

The whole process has made me have to rethink my "rules", but ditching my rules won't help. That would be like some cult leader saying, "Follow everything in the book ... except pages 14 and 73."

I guess I just have to learn to make my rules a little more flexible. That means red things can be washed with off-white things, right?

HOW TO MAKE A MORON: FIRST, ADD KIDS

It was a typical, "it's 3 p.m., here's what I did, here's what you need to do when you get home" kind of conversation.

" ... and I did the dishes and started the dishwasher, so you need to unload it when you get home."

I wasn't really paying attention. We men never pay attention to these kinds of phone calls. We aren't meant to. We only start listening when the topic gets around to sex, television, sports or alcohol. This is why the dishwasher never gets unloaded.

I usually toss in a few "uh-huhs" and "yeahs" to hold up my end of the conversation.

"uh-huh."

" ... and I didn't get the mail, so you better do that. Oh, I almost forgot to set the VCR to tape our shows."

The word "VCR" is very closely associated with "television" so I started to pay attention.

"No, honey," I said, remembering the last time my wife set the VCR and we ended up with three hours of "Designing Women" reruns. "I'll do it."

"... so, I will set the VCR, don't worry about it. I hope you have ..."

"No, I said I will set the VCR!"

" ... a nice day and I should be picking the boys ..."

"DEAR I SAID I WILL SET THE VCR!!!"

"... see you when I get home. Bye!"

She wasn't listening to me at all. I held the phone to my ear, listening to the silence as if she might pick it back up to apologize for hanging up on me. Then, I heard a voice ...

"If you would like to hear this message again, hit ..."

That's when I figured out that I had actually been carrying on a conversation with my voice mail. My brain had so far abandoned the rest of my body, I didn't remember hitting the button to retrieve my messages.

I could take this as a sign that senility is coming early or that my wife needs to stop leaving such long messages on my phone. Instead I chose to view this as one of my prime pieces of evidence that being a father make you stupid.

When I was growing up, I always thought my dad was a moron. Now, I know I was right.

All those sleepless nights and arguments that end in "Just do it because I said so" must take a toll on a parent's body and mind. The synapses in the brain must decide to take leave or go into an 18-year slumber.

After I moved out of my parent's house, I noticed my dad was getting smarter already. I thought it had to do with that old story about how the kid gets smarter and finally recognizes it in his father. That wasn't it.

For the years I was at home, my dad had no brain. I mean this was a guy who ran his own company, but still lost his 4-year-old son in the U.S. Capitol and once fell through the ceiling of our home because he forgot to step on the wood studs in the attic.

Only now that my own mental capacity is nearing zero do I realize the impact having children has. I have a short-term future of arguing with other parents over kid's soccer

.

games and using excuses like "you need to do it on your own" when my son asks me for help with homework I don't understand.

So, I am writing this little eulogy for my brain. I am already to the days of forgetting my sons' names, losing my car keys and standing in the shower trying to remember if I washed my hair already.

Could the years be far off when I will be wearing mismatching neon golf outfits even though I don't play golf or blaming my bodily noises on invisible animals?

I only hope that when my second son flies from the nest, my brain will come back because I am in the middle of a really good book right now, and I'd love to know how it turns out.

PLANNING IS PARENTS' FOLLY

Planning is a term parents like to use. We planned to have kids. We planned when they would arrive. And, if we were smart, we wouldn't plan anything again.

Mixing planning and children is like mixing Kool-Aid and poster paint, either way you end up with a mess.

But still we parents plan. My wife and I do it daily.

"What do you want to do tonight?" we ask each other.

This is a blissful moment because for a brief instant, we actually believe that we will get done whatever follows that question.

Take the other night for example. My wife answered my nightly question with, "Well, I'd like to do some bills and take a shower. If you could watch the kids while I do that then I'll give them a bath and we can get them in bed early for a change."

I said, "That would be great, because then I can write my column and get it in by the deadline for a change."

And we smiled at each other. It wasn't a contented smile. It was more like that smile you see on the faces of those people interviewed after having seen a UFO — happily out of touch with reality.

This is how the night really went:

6:05 p.m. — Mom attempts to leave the room to pay bills. Son No. 1 tries to help Son No. 2 into his highchair and drops him on his head. Both boys start crying and screaming for their mother. (It's not that both boys wanted their mom. They both instinctively knew that she was the one who would be most inconvenienced so she becomes the target. It's kind of like a "grass is always greener"-thing.)

6:12 p.m. — Boys have settled down. Mom sneaks out again while Dad brings dinner to the table. Fighting and crying ensue as both boys make it very clear their choice for tonight's entree is glazed doughnut holes.

6:16 p.m. — Each boy eats an atom or two of dinner and then screams for doughnuts.

6:19 p.m. — Dad, through gritted teeth, tells the boys to be quiet and if they will just calm down they can have all the doughnuts they want, but they can't tell Mom.

6:29 p.m. — Son No. 1, after eating twice his body weight in fried dough, calls to his mom to tell her about the doughnuts.

6:30 p.m. — Mom gives Dad look of death.

6:31 p.m. — Dad gives Son No. 1 look of death.

6:32 p.m. — Son No. 1 sticks out his tongue and gives a Bronx cheer.

6:40 p.m. — Dad decides he needs some help and utters the phrase that has saved parental sanity for generations: "Let's watch TV."

6:45 p.m. — Dad surfs through the channels by remote at lightning speed. Son No. 1 and No. 2 both scream out as he passes by a channel with ultra violent cartoons. Dad goes back. Kids zone out. Life is good.

7:15 p.m. — Mom, suspicious of the quiet, investigates to find some furry character being impaled on the screen. Another look of death. Bills will have to be put off again.

7:30 p.m. — Boys convinced to take a bath with the enticement of getting to run around naked. Parents thought it was a good idea, but now can't catch kids.

7:45 p.m. — Parents decided boys aren't THAT dirty and decide to skip a bath and to simply get pajamas on and head for an early bedtime.

8 p.m. — Yeah... right!

8:15 p.m. — Both boys in pajamas, they are wrangled to bed where Dad will read three books ("And we're only reading three tonight!") while Mom tries once again to take care of the bills.

8:45 p.m. — Dad finishes seventh book and he is about to pass out when both boys sit straight up and yell, "SNACK!"

8:46 p.m. — "No, you already ate. No snack!"

(You know the drill)

9:30 p.m. — Snack.

9:35 p.m. — Boys placed back in bed but insist on practicing for the 2015 Summer Olympic Bed Jumping competition.

9:45 p.m. — Both boys finally are lying down.

9:46 p.m. — 4-year-old: "I have to poop!" and 2-year-old takes off his pajamas, diaper and pees on the floor.

11:15 p.m. — Boys again lying down in bed. Parents are nearly comatose.

11:16 p.m. — "Read us another book."

11:45 p.m. — After five more books, kids are finally starting to tire out and eventually fall asleep.

Midnight — Both boys asleep for 1.2 seconds before Son No. 2 bolts up in bed and screams like a banshee.

1 a.m. — Time no longer relevant. Parents on fifth night with no sleep and boys are on their second wind of the day.

2:17 a.m. — Boys finally out. Parents in bed staring at the ceiling in anticipation of the next waking event. They can't sleep, so they do what all parents do in such a situation: plan what they won't get done tomorrow.

JOINT VENTURES

GOING THROUGH SPELL AND BACK

I was in seventh grade.

Everyone from the whole school was staring at me. The room was absolutely silent except for the low hum from the microphone in front of me.

"Can you say that word again, please?" I begged, trying to buy some time for my brain to somehow figure out how to spell that darn word.

"The word is (some indecipherable sound that I am still not sure was English). You have 15 seconds."

All of the other kids from my class were looking at me like I was somebody who couldn't spell his way out of a paper bag, even though I had easily won our class spelling bee and I was a favorite to take the school title.

And this was the first word. Nobody loses on the first word. The first round is where they give you the spelling equivalent of 2 + 2.

But I had no idea how to spell the word "gaudy". I swear that before that day, I had never heard of "gaudy." Just about every day since, when I hear that word I re-member that day of shame when I spelled it G-O-D-D-Y.

Since that moment, I have hated spelling.

I couldn't see any reason for learning how to spell words. That's what spell check is for. And it is only through the magic of spell check that I was able to become a writer. I have been out of school for many years now and I finally discovered the reason for learning how to spell: kids.

My son is almost 2. This means he can run, leap, crawl and dig in places 2-year-olds were never intended to be.

He can also talk. That means he can understand things that his mother and I never intended him to hear.

It started one night many months ago. My son had fallen asleep in his mother's arms with a half-eaten cookie still in his hand. Once my son decides to sleep (which isn't that often) we are usually able to have a discussion without waking him up.

I asked my wife, "Do you want me to grab the cookie?"

Well I found out that "cookie" is a word that is apparently hard-wired into every kid's brain and it will alert them even if they are sound asleep.

"COOKIE," my son screamed out of his slumber. "MY COOKIE. MY COOKIE." He was then so wired up and fearful that his dad was going to steal his cookie, he didn't nod off again for several hours.

Fortunately, cookie is a pretty easy word to spell, so now when my wife tells me to hide the "C-O-O-K-I-E-S," it doesn't take me very long to figure out what she wants.

But now my son is getting smarter. He knows plenty of words. And — darn it — he knows big words.

So this is how life in our house is now:

My wife: "Can you get the C-A-N-T-A-L-O-U-P-E out of the fridge so he can have a S-N-A-C-K before he goes to S-L-E-E-P? And don't go D-O-W-N-S-T-A-I-R-S because he will want to watch T-E-L-E-V-I-S-I-O-N ."

Me (after a long, confused pause): "Why do you want a C-A-T-E-R-P-I-L-L-A-R?"

I have to admit my spelling bee days are coming back to haunt me. (And, in case you are wondering, my wife knows how to spell "gaudy".)

For now this little code system seems to be working. But I know my son will soon be figuring out what we are talking about.

At that point I will have to go back to my school days again and use yet another thing that I thought was useless when I was in high school: foreign language.

How do you say cookie in French anyway?

OUT OF THE MOUTHS OF BABES

It was a typical Friday rush hour. The highest areas of traffic were not on the interstate or heading out of town for a weekend outing.

Nope, most of the folks were at the video store, including my 2-year-old son and me. My son knows the video store very well because that is where Robin Hood, Tarzan, Buzz Lightyear and all his other favorite characters live.

We were working our way into a parking spot. A couple in a large car moved glacially in front of us while waiting to find the perfect parking place. And just as I was about to say something, I heard a voice from the back of my car.

"C'mon, let's get going people."

OK, so my son probably didn't pick that line up watching "Sesame Street." He is at that age where he mimics just about everything he hears. And he's really good at it.

This is the time I feared most as a parent. You see, I don't really have the cleanest mouth in the world. I have been known to use four-letter words to describe everything from the idiots on the road to a really i@*$%-ing sunset.

In my defense, I have really improved. Since my son came along, I have limited my vocabulary to mostly PG-level, which is a big leap from NC-17.

But there are times when you have to say something, especially when driving. I learned this from my dad. He drove more with his mouth than with his hands. As a kid, I always thought that if my dad ever lost his voice, he would never be able to drive again. And I have carried on that tradition. Most of the time, I don't even realize I'm doing it. But my son does.

"Daddy, why is that guy a moron?" he once asked from his car seat observing post.

"Well, son, there is a little thing called a turn signal which that guy apparently doesn't know how to use. And he's going 5 mph under the speed limit. That's what a moron is."

That was the best description I could think of so that he wouldn't duplicate my language when he got to daycare.

I have this nightmare that my son will be playing with another kid on a tricycle and my son will say something like, "You idiot. Who taught you how to drive that thing?"

I am trying to control my mouth while in the car, but my son is a master at picking out the exact thing I don't want him to repeat and using it against me.

The other day we were at the store. Like most children, my son is curious and he expressed this curiosity by asking the question, "Watcha doin', Daddy?" at least 10 times every minute.

"We are going to pick up some bananas."

"OOOOhhhh." This is his standard response. It works well because it makes it sound like he was listening to what I was saying. I guess it's the toddler equivalent of the husband's motto: "Yes, Dear."

He continued with his questions as we went through the produce section, canned foods section, deli and the cereal aisles.

"Oh, your daddy's a dummy," I told him, before he could ask why we were suddenly backtracking. "I forgot to get apples. We will have to go back."

After that lengthy session in the store, which included fascinating lessons about things my son had never seen before, (i.e. kitty litter, cake mix and guacamole) the only thing my son got out of the trip was the word "dummy."

It came up when I saw my son playing with another little boy.

"I'm not a dummy. You're a dummy."

"I'm not a dummy. You're a dummy."

My son countered with the only logical thing he could think of: "I'm not a dummy. I'm a boy."

GOING HOME

The fantasy was always the same.

I wasn't running fast. I was never a big fan of running fast. No, it was more like a home run trot. I rounded each base at a slow, steady clip. The Major League fans cheered. As I rounded third, I picked up the pace and my journey culminated in a big two-footed leap on home plate.

The only thing standing in the way of that fantasy ever becoming a reality is my basic lack of physical ability.

Despite that, I always kept the fantasy. I cheered and high-fived as I watched professional ballplayers jog nonchalantly around the base paths — but with every cheer was a bit of envy.

My day finally came a few weeks ago at a Colorado Rockies game. I took my 2-year-old son to the ball game.

It was only after we bought the tickets — I swear — that I discovered it was a "run the bases" day. That meant that kids could come onto the field after the game and live out my fantasy — minus the stadium-clearing home run hit, of course.

My son was ready to run from the minute the game started.

"Do I get to run now?" he asked.

"No, Larry Walker gets to go now."

"But Larry Walker already went," my son said.

I had no reply so I bought him a $15 ice cream sundae. As the end of the game neared, I got more and more excited. Yeah, this event was for the kids, but I had a 2-year-old and nobody would expect a 2-year-old to run the bases without his dad.

We made our way to the registration table. My son started to get sleepy. As we waited with a couple hundred other kids and parents, my son rested his head on my shoulder.

Oh, great. This was going to look good. A dad jogs around the bases while his son sleeps in his arms. I think it would have been a little too obvious. If I was any kind of father, I would have driven home right then, but I was on a mission.

Finally we were led through the stadium toward home plate. My son rubbed his eyes and looked around. I swear I didn't wake him up.

As we waited for the first kids to run, I asked an employee if dads could run with little kids. Three other dads in hearing range and I cheered when she said we could.

Ahead of us, one of those dads took off running with his son. At that point, my son made up his mind.

"I'm running," he said with the stern look that only 2-year-olds can make. "You're not running."

With that, I set him down and he took off running — my fantasy completely shattered.

I know I'm biased, but my son had great form as he glided around the diamond. His elbows pumped. His head was held high. And his legs — well, they didn't move too quickly.

Heck, he's only 2.

He plodded along as other bigger kids lapped him. The people remaining in the stands began to notice my son — he was wearing a bright green shirt — and they began to cheer him on.

"GO GREEN KID!" they yelled.

The roar — well, that's how it sounded to me — grew to a crescendo as my son finally rounded third and headed for home. It reached ovation volume when he hit home.

I was yelling and screaming (and taking a lot of pictures). I lifted my son up like he'd just won the World Series. Other kids were giving him high fives and parents told me how neat it was to watch the little guy run.

As we made it to our car, people who had been watching from the stands came over to congratulate my son and me. My son beamed and told everyone that he was a big boy because he ran the bases by himself.

I was beaming, too.

It's amazing how on the day my fantasy died, I fulfilled one I never knew I had.

DOWN THE TUBES

Most parents won't admit it, but part of the fun of having kids is the feeling of power.

Oh, sure, that feeling is fleeting and not based in any sort of reality, but there is a sense of being in power over a young child whose mind you can mold to learn the things you want them to.

If you want John Lennon to be the 34th president of the United States, just tell your young child that. Your child will hate you later when he fails history, but you were able to change history for that brief moment.

I love being my children's encyclopedia. I love that when my son asks me a question, he believes my answer — no matter how far off the mark I am.

I know this time will be brief. Soon my son will realize that I am as stupid as the rest of the people in the world, but I want to maintain this sense of awe from my son for as long as possible.

One of the more memorable moments in my childhood was when my dad took my sister and me to learn to ski for the first time. My dad had never skied either, so he was taking lessons with us. Watching my dad make the same mistakes I made brought about a revelation that my dad didn't know everything — and I figured that out just from looking at the stupid outfit he wore on the slopes.

Sure, that moment also taught me that since my dad struggled to learn like I did, that maybe there was hope for me. But that was also when I learned he was fallible (and fall-able).

I am not at the place (OK, I'm not mature enough, maybe) when I want my son to know what I don't know. This time is short and I want to enjoy it.

So, when we went to the mountains just before the holidays, I had to decide if it was time for my son to see his dad be an idiot. If he saw me on skis, I was dead. Even though I have been skiing for years, you would never know it by watching me on the slopes.

My main skiing technique involves an excessive amount of yelling the phrase, "Outta the way." I wasn't ready for my son to see that.

So, instead of skiing, I took my son snow tubing.

For those who don't know, snow tubing is the act of flying down a snowy hill on an inner tube. This practice has been done for years, but now the ski resorts have taken the only aspect of the activity that involved any physical exertion — the climb back up the hill — and installed a towrope.

In other words, it is my ideal sport. If snow tubing were an Olympic sport, I could easily bring home the gold.

I knew my son would like this activity because, well, he's a guy and anytime a guy can go REALLY fast and REAL-LY out of control and REALLY almost die, we love it.

I was in a no-lose situation. I was going to show my son how to do the one physical activity I can do beyond flipping channels on the remote. I was in my element and my son was going to get to revel in my glory.

When we got to the top of the mountain, my son's eyes were huge. He was so excited watching the other tubers (that's my lingo which I think really impressed my son) fly down the different runs. The runs basically went straight down the slope and then curved at the bottom so the tube rode on the side wall like a bobsled.

The runs were obviously separated into advanced, intermediate and beginner runs with the easiest one closest to the towrope. But at the top, I noticed a fourth run, that nobody was using, even closer to the rope. I figured this would be the easiest run and thought it would be perfect for my son's first attempt.

He sat in his tube. I sat in mine while I held his tube close to me — and then we were off. We started going faster and faster. The part of the guy's brain that wants to ALMOST die during these thrills started to get worried that we really WOULD die.

We came barreling toward the turn at the bottom and I realized the bank was not going to be big enough to keep us in. I realized this as we went flying over the bank at 110 mph. My 3-year-old son flew out of his tube into the air and landed headfirst in a snow bank.

Apparently (according to the many worried ski resort workers who ran over to check on us) that "easy" run wasn't really a run. It was supposed to catch any tubes that fell off the towrope so they wouldn't hurt anyone.

So, yes, I figured out a way to screw up snow tubing and a way for me to look like a moron at a ski resort — in front of my eldest son.

Fortunately, my son pulled his head from the snow and giggled. "I want to go again," he said loudly.

And we went again — down the correct run, from then on. My son was disappointed that we didn't crash again.

Apparently, crashing is pretty cool for a 3-year-old.

And if that's true my son will think I'm really cool next year when I take him skiing.

UP IN THE AIR

Because I occasionally write about my two boys in this column, I get some feedback from parents who have been through the 1- and 3-year-old stages. They make sure I realize that no matter how frantic life is now, it only gets worse.

"You have no idea."

"You just wait..."

"You think it's tough now? You'll see."

But most of these comments are from moms. Moms treasure the "baby" years. As their babies get old enough to tell them they don't want a hug right now or don't want to wear the orange jumper no matter how "GORGEOUS" it is, moms long for those quiet moments when they held a helpless infant and cuddled for hours.

Veteran moms tell me that no matter how crazy life is now, it gets worse as the kids get more independence. One woman was practically in tears as she told me about the first time her son rode his bike out of the driveway and into a lifetime of troubles boys always find on bikes.

"You think you have sleepless nights now," another woman told me. "Wait until you are waiting for them to come home from their first high school dance. That's a sleepless night!"

For all of these wonderful insights and predictions for a worrisome future, I am thankful. But I have to tell you, like most dads I can't wait for my boys to grow up.

Guys around babies are like guys at their first non-parental party — they don't really know what to do and they know that even if they do it right, they are probably still going to get spit up on.

Watch a dad with a baby. Yeah, we will make all the silly faces and we will act warm and fuzzy, but what we are really thinking is: "This kid should start to learn to throw a ball NOW. The kid across the street can already belch and scratch himself. My kid can't even throw a decent fastball." But we dads also know there are moms in the world who want to keep their "babies" as babies for as long as possible.

That is why our attempts to "help" our children grow up sooner must be kept secret. This is why when mommy is away, dad pulls out his rust-covered Erector set (for ages 11 and up) and gives it to a 1-year-old.

Sometimes we just have to move the rather slow growing process along.

That was the idea behind the event that almost forced me to leave my youngest child in McDonald's forever.

My youngest is 1 and a half. That half is important because if you round it off, he is 2, which means he's more than two-thirds of the way to 3. And three is the minimum age on the playground equipment that nearly became his lifelong home. (My wife pointed out the minimum age requirements at one of our subsequent trips to McDonald's. I mean, who really READS those things?)

My oldest loves the playground at McDonald's. He can spend hours in those bright tubes and slides. And the real reason parents take kids there anyway is to tire them out so we parents can finally get some sleep.

I figured that if one kid gets so tired from the playground, it would be even better if two did. So, during our most recent trip to McDonald's (without Mom) I turned them loose on the playground. In my defense, I really didn't think the 1-year-old could climb that high.

I just turned for a second. My oldest wanted to show me a death-defying move on another part of the playground. When I looked back, all I saw was my youngest's legs.

I probably could have caught him. But I thought about that woman watching her son ride away on his bike and I had conflicting thoughts: "Cool, now I can sit here and eat my fries" and "My wife is gonna kill me."

Modern fast food playgrounds are very high. I don't know exactly why. All it really does is leave a lot of parents standing below yelling their child's name as the kid laughs and says he will never come down.

I stood there (eating my fries) with the other parents, staring at the elevated playground like a group of gawkers waiting for some guy to jump out an office-building window.

My oldest came down the slide and I told him to go back up and make sure his brother was OK. Two minutes later, my oldest was down and said my youngest wasn't up there.

Of course, I could hear my youngest giggle like the cackle of the Phantom of the McDonald's Playground.

Some other kids also came down and said they couldn't see my youngest.

And I was trying to figure out if it would be better to explain to my wife how I lost our son or how the firefighters had to free my fat butt from a bright yellow tube during a failed rescue attempt.

Finally, he came down on his own. He immediately tried to go right back up. But I grabbed him, hugged him and decided there was plenty of time in the future for him to be old enough to terrify me again.

For now, I'll enjoy my baby, too.

FASHION SENSELESS

My wife and I are both professionals. What this means is that we do a lot of work that doesn't require a lot of heavy lifting. What it doesn't mean is that we look the part.

In a perfect world, we would be able to do our jobs — effectively and efficiently — while being dressed like truck drivers. But that's not the way the world works.

I have moaned before about my lack of fashion literacy and my wife suffers from a less fatal version of the same disease. So, when I was told in a not-so-subtle way recently at work that I needed to improve my look (it went something like "You dress like a color-blind homeless person."), I asked my boss to show me the ways of the fashion world. She had no idea it was a lost cause.

What really makes me sad is that my fashion stupidity has rubbed off on my son who has the preschool version of fashionitis. While I shopped with my boss, I kept thinking of a recent conversation I had with my son ...

BOSS: These pants are perfect.

ME: They look just like the pants I'm wearing.

BOSS: Those are khakis. These are slacks.

ME: They look the same to me.

BOSS: Feel them. They are much different.
ME: But who's going to be feeling my legs?
BOSS: These are polyester. Those are cotton.
ME: So, I should wear the ones that aren't comfortable?
BOSS: Now, you're getting it.

ME: You can't wear pajamas to school.
SON: Why not?
ME: Because that's not what we wear to school.
SON: My pajamas are just like my pants I wear to school.
ME: No, they are not. The pajama pants are softer.
SON: That's why I like them.
ME: You need to wear the uncomfortable pants.

BOSS: This black shirt is hideous. (Pointing) But this one is perfect.
ME: They look the same.
BOSS: Are you an idiot? This is business attire. And that one is just ugly.
ME: OK

ME: OK, so let's pick out a new shirt. How about this?
SON: It looks just like my pajama top.
ME: But, it's not a pajama top. So, you can wear it.
SON: (Silence followed by a look that told me he thought I was an idiot.)

ME: How about this shirt?
BOSS: Fine, if you want to look like a pimp.

ME: How about this shirt?
SON: (Pointing to the ugly orange and red shirt he loves) I want that one.
ME: Fine.
BOSS: And you need shiny shoes.
ME: What's the matter with these?

BOSS: They aren't shiny.

ME: I can shine them.

BOSS: If you aren't even going to try, why am I here?

ME: Go get your shoes.

SON: I want to wear my dress-up shoes.

ME: But you're just going to school. Don't you want to get comfortable shoes?

SON: I like these. They're shiny.

ME: How about you go to my office and I'll go to your school?

SON: OK.

FISHING FOR
A WAY OUT

As a father, I want to be there to teach my sons about all the manly things in this world. Baseball. Burping. Spitting. You know, all the stuff that boys need (and WANT) to know.

But I have recently come to two conclusions:

First, my sons have been able to burp louder than me from birth.

Second, there is one area of manly activity with which I am simply unable to assist them: fishing.

I have never been a big fan of fishing. I remember going on a number of fishing expeditions with my dad and they were all great — except for the fishing part.

I'm not really sure why I don't like fishing. Perhaps it has something to do with taking a living animal from a place where it is rather comfortable and then killing it and slathering it with tartar sauce for dinner. (I like my fish from Mrs. Paul's, thank you!)

But I don't think that's the reason. I wasn't able to figure out the problem until I broke down the pieces of a fishing trip:

- Getting up early and going to some place where there's water? Well, that's not too bad.
- Casting a line in the water and waiting for a nibble? Actually, this is probably the best part ... especially because older fishermen get to bring beer on their outings!
- And then getting a bite, reeling it in and touching the slimy, flapping thing to get it off the hook and then slicing it up to eat it? Yup! We have a winner!

That's the problem with fishing: Catching the fish!

My sons have always been fascinated with fishing. When they were younger, I was able to feed their curiosity and avoid slimy fish by buying those plastic fishing poles with magnetic fish for them to play with in our plastic wading pool in the backyard.

That's not good enough anymore.

Recently we went to my parents' house in California. My parents live by a lake that is crammed with fish of the non-plastic variety. Fortunately, my sons also have my brother-in-law (their uncle), Mark, who would pretty much rather be fishing than doing just about anything else.

When we arrived at my parents' house for a two-week vacation, Uncle Mark had purchased plastic tackle boxes for both of my sons. Tackle boxes are apparently like catnip for my sons. I suppose it's the really sharp hooks and rubbery lures that are the draw.

My boys were pleading with Uncle Mark for a fishing trip and he happily obliged. Within a few minutes, my oldest boy had already reeled in a large catfish and he loved every minute of it.

"Can we cut it open and see the bones?"

"I want to see the brain!"

I worry about my sons.

Uncle Mark decided this fish was going to go back in the water because it had some sharp parts on its fins that could hurt kids, but later when they caught a big ol' bass, he thought it would be good to show them what's inside.

"I want the eyeball!"

"I want to see the brain!"

In case you are wondering, while all this was going on, I was averting my eyes and thinking wistfully of the next lesson I had planned for my sons on how to make farting noises with your armpit.

A few days later, we were all swimming in the lake. Uncle Mark had dropped a few lines with bobbers on them in the water and then left to run some errands.

And, of course, we saw the bobber go down. And then we heard the WHIRRRR of the line as a fish took off with the bait.

I yelled, "Mark! You got another fish!"

No response. WHIRRRRR.

"MARK!!! COME GET YOUR FISH!!!"

My son went over and started to reel in the fish (which he did very well). And we soon saw it was another catfish — even bigger and meaner looking than the first one!

"MARK!!!"

I had a number of conflicting thoughts going through my brain that left me completely paralyzed:

- It's slimy.
- Your sons are watching. Do something!
- Mark said something about sharp things, right?
- It's slimy.

I wish I had thought fast enough to explain to my sons that because I didn't have a fishing license, I couldn't get the fish out of the water, but instead I froze and, finally, Uncle Mark came to the rescue — although part of me wanted him to get poked by whatever those sharp things are.

As we left for home, Uncle Mark made sure both boys took their tackle boxes.

"Be sure to have your dad take you fishing," he said.

I figure I can stall for one more year by pretending there are no places to fish in Colorado. When the boys catch on, Uncle Mark better plan on coming out here for a visit.

I HATE IT WHEN THAT HAPPENS

"MINI" AND "NAKED" DON'T GO TOGETHER

I wasn't naked ... I swear!

If you were one of the seemingly millions of people who saw a large bearded naked man driving a minivan across town last week, I would like to assure you there is a simple explanation.

It happened when my wife and I were going to pick our children up from their grandmother's house where they were enjoying some time with grandma while my wife and I were enjoying the fact grandma lives in Greeley.

I was at my mother-in-law's house, holding my youngest son, when he decided to greet me by throwing up his last 17 meals on my chest.

For those of you who don't have children, you may not realize that kids don't really need a reason to throw up. Heck, I think they do it sometimes when they are just bored.

Rookie parents will call the doctor immediately. The doctor will tell them it isn't a big deal unless they do it a couple of times an hour. And these rookie parents will watch the clock and they will notice their child will wait at least 90 minutes before puking again — unless Scooby-Doo is on. No child will throw up when Scooby is on.

My wife and I aren't exactly rookies. We know that all you can do is clean up the mess and stay out of firing range for the next 90 minutes.

But, I digress. Anyway, because we were at my mother-in-law's house, I didn't have a new shirt to put on.

So, I decided to drive without my shirt on — that's it.

I have driven shirtless before. But on those previous occasions I was driving a pickup truck or my old 1978 Chevy Nova. People don't even give a second look to a shirtless guy in a pickup. Heck, if you are driving a Chevy Nova with a shirt on, you get funny glances.

But a minivan is different.

The minivan has taken quite a beating over the years. Some people feel they are officially old when they finally give into the minivan pressure. Other people feel the mini-van signals the end of frivolity and spontaneity and marks the beginning of a life directed toward soccer practices and hunting down Popsicle sticks for school projects.

Of course, all these people are correct.

I thought I had come to terms with those things a year ago, when we bought the minivan. What I didn't realize was how differently people look at you in a minivan.

When I learned to drive, I had my Chevy Nova. The look you get when you are driving a Nova is fear. People realize that if you are driving a car that ugly, you aren't going to really worry about damaging it by causing a 14-car pileup just for the fun of it.

But in a minivan, you are seen as safe. Minivans signal. Minivans let other drivers cut them off without any obscene hand gestures. Minivans always yield to the car on the right and never go more than 3 mph over the limit (this reckless speed is only allowed when late for a Boy Scout meeting).

And minivans are NOT driven by fat shirtless men. In fact, any man not wearing a shirt in a minivan must also not be wearing pants. Other drivers can't prove this because the minivan is so tall, but it is assumed. In other words, naked minivan drivers must be perverts. That was exactly the look I got from the other drivers as I made my way home. I can handle people looking at me strangely, but since Lady Luck doesn't smile on shirtless minivan drivers, the first car I passed was — and this is SO true — my boss.

Yes, the man who has control of my paycheck was the first to gawk at the bare-chested freak in the minivan. You can't tell me that image won't come up when it's time for my annual review!

So, that's my explanation. It's all very simple. It's all very believable.

OK, forget it.

STORAGE SPACE OR MUSEUM?

I'm pretty sure my mom never, and I mean ever, threw away anything from when I was a kid.

Somewhere in the vast array of boxes my mom stored in the attic — the same boxes my dad had to circumnavigate every year to get the Christmas decorations down — she stored every piece of my childhood memorabilia.

Don't believe me? When my first son was born, my mom sent a bouquet of flowers to the hospital — in the same baby-blue elephant vase she had received flowers in when I was born. And she also sent me the outfit I wore when she brought me home from the hospital.

Still think I'm lying? When my second son was born, she sent a bouquet in another vase she had received at my birth, and she included my first baby rattle!

Not convinced? When I got married, she gave my wife a note I had written to my parents — at age 12 — explaining I wouldn't be home until later and where I would be. Apparently, mom saved it because I had signed it "sincerly" — she loved the formality and the misspelling.

More proof? She also gave my wife a scrawny, ugly cutting board I had made for my mom in eighth-grade woodshop. I had sanded it down so much it was completely unusable for its intended purpose, but my mom had used if for years as a coaster for her morning coffee.

Anyway, my point is that every conceivable souvenir from my youth was stored in that attic and apparently cataloged in my mom's brain.

I never really understood the skill and willpower that such an endeavor requires. Now that I have two children and a comparable amount of storage space, I am noticing just how impressive this feat was.

A good example of my lack of skill at being the historic custodian of my children's youth is their toy box.

All parents know that toys — like weeds or unwanted visiting relatives—will continue to grow and take over a house unless they are carefully trimmed every so often.

This, I am convinced, is the reason young children take naps. It is the only time parents can go through the toy box and remove the old and broken toys. And when I say remove, I don't mean, "throw out," because parents must remember their role as curator of their child's museum. So we fill a box with "memorable toys" and then we throw the others in the trash.

In the "memorable" box are the toys you hope to show them before they go off to college or before they get married. These are the toys that have a really good story to accompany them. We can pull these toys out, later, at a critical juncture in their lives to embarrass them and remind them that they will always be "our baby."

In this, my mom excelled and I stink. The absolute moment I throw out a toy that is broken, useless or hasn't been played with in the last year is the exact moment when one of my sons asks for said toy and goes into hysterics when I can't produce it.

Toys may seem the most unmanageable part of the curator role, but it's not even close. The worst part is the artwork! The guy who runs the Louvre in France doesn't have to make decisions that could send a small child into a lifetime of counseling. Parents do!

You see, parents have a limited amount of gallery space. Children have an unlimited ability to produce things they feel should be put on display for the entire world to see.

I'm not talking about just the family refrigerator space, either. Although that is considered prime real estate and both my boys are giddy when one of their pieces is selected for such an honor.

I also look at the workspaces of some of my co-workers. They are surrounded by artwork created by their children because their home museums have overflowed.

It's the selection process I hate. My son will bring home from daycare a huge piece of construction paper on which will be glued a single cotton ball. This is art. And it is to be appreciated.

However, there's a part of my brain that believes my child's daycare throws nothing away. Instead, they have children glue all of the leftover paper scraps, odds and ends and other garbage to construction paper and send it home as art so we have to deal with it. It's really a pretty clever idea.

My wife started a box of this art for each of the boys, but those boxes were overflowing after the first week of her project. The simple fact of the matter is that we have to chuck some of it out.

That means that now I — as the parent — have to throw out a piece of paper with a tiny blue crayon mark in the upper left corner despite the fact that may have been the expression of my son's heart and soul poured onto the page. Or he may have just dropped the crayon on the paper as he tried to shove the crayon into his mouth.

I get to decide.

Or maybe we just need more storage space.

WALKING THROUGH LIFE

It's been said that you should make sure you smell the flowers as you walk through life.

In other words, you shouldn't focus totally on the destination so that you forget about enjoying the journey.

This is pretty good advice — unless you are REALLY late for work or something like that.

I've tried to instill this concept in my sons. I point out interesting things while we are driving and they seem to have grasped the concept and taken it to a whole new level.

In fact, my oldest son is pretty much a flower-smelling expert.

I first discovered this on a family walk around the neighborhood.

I suppose I should preface all of this by saying I am not a big fan of the "family walk." Walking is something that I feel strongly should be done from the sofa to the fridge and from the parking lot to someplace you need to go. Walking is something that should be done only when it is impossible to drive.

Going for a "walk" never made much sense to me. I mean, yes, I believe you should smell the flowers as you walk through life, but I also strongly believe you shouldn't "walk" through life.

But my wife is a big backer of the "walk" so we "walk."

My oldest son, however, may have a few more of my genes than those of my wife, because he's not much into walking either. In fact, he can't walk more than three or four steps in a row without stopping to point out some interesting thing on the sidewalk.

"Daddy, look! It's a worm!"

"Yeah, I know. It looks a lot like the worm you saw four feet ago."

Step. Step. Step.

"Mommy, look at this! What is that?"

"That's a rock, dear."

"Cool. I like rocks."

Anyway, this continues over the next four hours as we finally make it back home after going around our block once.

From the first day my wife forced me to "walk," I have dreamed of ways to get out of it. And as my oldest son turned 4 years old, I discovered my salvation: a bike.

A bike is a kid's key to freedom and fun at high speeds and far away from home. And I knew my wife wouldn't let my son go by himself, so I got to go on my bike with him.

No more walks for me.

Soon my son and I prepared for our first good bike ride. We put on our helmets and practiced pedaling and braking in the driveway before heading out.

My wife was scared to death.

I told her to take a walk to relax. She did.

I let my son lead the way as we cruised up our street. The wind blew through his hair as he pedaled faster and faster.

SCREECH!

He stopped.

I wasn't paying much attention and I plowed my bike into the back of his.

"Why'd you stop?"

"Look, Daddy. Aren't those cool flowers?"

"Huh? We're riding here. Yes, they're cool flowers, but let's get moving. We have a whole world to see."

But my son's world is different from mine. He is fascinated by ... well, everything.

That's the way our bike ride went.

Pedal. Pedal. Pedal. SCREECH.

By the time we finally got back to the house, I was exhausted and we had only ridden a few blocks. The stop and start was killing me and I was already trying to figure out how to make blinders for my son so he couldn't see off to the side.

My wife, however, was looking relaxed and rested from her walk.

Guess that goes to show me something, huh?

Yup, it's time to teach my son to drive a car!

SANTA PLUS BROCCOLI EQUALS PEACE

Santa is a parent's best friend.

Don't get me wrong. I thought the jolly ol' fat guy was pretty darn cool when I was a kid, too. I was obsessed with Santa as a kid.

When my mom took me to the mall to sit on Santa's lap, it was like meeting the ultimate celebrity. I rehearsed in my room exactly what I was going to say to him.

As I waited in line, the other kids would fight and play. I just stared at Santa. He mesmerized me.

I also fully believed that Santa could see everything. The way I figured it, if he could tell when I didn't eat the broccoli on my dinner plate at home, he wouldn't have any problems seeing me pick a fight in line as I waited to give him my list.

Santa just has that kind of pull. And that's what parents love.

I never knew the true force of Santa until I saw how Santa affected my two sons. They are struck with the same obsession I had as a child, and as the parent, I use it to my full advantage.

I know that there are some people who believe Santa shouldn't be a part of Christmas because it is a religious holiday. But, for a 4-year-old kid, what do you think is a better motivator for being good: eternal damnation or not getting a 4x4 remote control truck that does flips and plays music?

Santa is the best way I have found to control my kids. I begin invoking his name about nine months before Christmas.

"Now, you remember last Christmas when you got that Buzz Lightyear from Santa because you were a good boy? Do you think Santa would like it if he knew you were being mean to your little brother? Maybe he won't bring you any toys this year."

This speech is ALWAYS followed by at least 10 minutes of good behavior. Non-parents may think 10 minutes isn't much, but those 10 minutes can be the difference between sanity and wanting to jingle my son's bells.

As Christmas gets closer, my speech gets shorter and the period of good behavior seems to last longer.

In fact, now that we're in the final stretch and my son already sees the presents under the tree, all I have to do is look up and say, "Hey, Santa, did you see that? Guess we might be adding one to the 'naughty' list!"

My son then immediately stops doing whatever bad thing he was doing and asks me to tell Santa that he is a good boy.

This year is the first year my youngest son has been able to grasp the concept of Santa and I wanted to make sure the idea stuck for as long as possible. I told him how good boys get toys and good presents from Santa and bad boys get coal in their stockings.

My oldest son overheard this conversation and even though he had heard me say it before, something about it hit him funny this time.

"What's coal, Daddy?"

"It's a gross black rock that gets messes everywhere. Yuck!"

"Daddy, I want a black rock. I want a mess. I want coal!" My youngest started in on the chant. "COAL! COAL! COAL!"

I had to think fast. I was losing my lone chance at peace (even just 10 minutes at a time) so I grabbed the only thing I could think of and I made up a new Christmas tradition.

"If Santa knows you want coal, he won't bring it for bad boys. Instead, you know what they get?"

"WHAT?!?!" my sons asked.

"Broccoli!"

Needless to say, I'm back in the driver's seat and my sons are doing everything they can to stay in Santa's good graces.

COACH HAS TO HAVE CLIPBOARD

To be a coach you must have three things: a whistle, a clipboard and a desire to yell for no reason whatsoever.

I have no idea what the clipboard is for, but it looks important and all the other coaches have one, so it must be vital. As for the whistle, well, ... I guess it makes you look official.

So, I guess all you really need to be a coach is the ability to be loud for no reason.

Watch any professional sports coach on TV. He is in a stadium with 30,000 people who are all yelling. And what does he do? He yells at his players as if they could actually hear him among the cheers from the stands.

And then he looks at his clipboard (I gotta figure out what that's all about).

It may sound easy. But when you put all your energy into short succinct phrases so you can yell them at players, you want them to be heard. A professional coach knows this doesn't happen.

How does one develop this skill?

Youth sports.

This year I began my professional coach-in-training program by accepting the challenge to coach my oldest son's co-ed soccer team, which is composed of 4- and 5-year-olds.

After a long season, I can truly say that I am an expert at being ignored.

In fact, I am pretty sure that even after a number of games and tons of practices, at least nine of my ten players wouldn't even know who the coach of their team is (my son included).

Here's how our season went:

FIRST WEEK —
"OK, guys, how many of you know the rules of soccer?"
Nothing.
"OK, well, first thing is you kick the ball..."
A hand pops up.
"Yes?"
"Are we done yet?"

SECOND WEEK —
"I want everyone to stand on this line... no THIS line ... That's a circle ... THIS is a line. Please stand here..."
Imagine a small bowl. Now imagine trying to arrange 10 marbles in a line on the curved bottom of that bowl.
"OK, let's stand on the circle..."

THIRD WEEK —
I figured that since nobody was paying attention, I should use my whistle to get their attention and then they would listen to me.
TWEEEEET!
"OK, everyone, today we are ..."
"Can I blow your whistle?"
"Can you play a song on that thing?"
"Play Twinkle Little Star!"

I HATE IT WHEN THAT HAPPENS

FOURTH WEEK —

It's time to put all that practice into action on the playing field. Since I can't be on the field with them, I revert to yelling for communication.

"Kick the ball"

"No!! The OTHER WAY!"

"That's OK, we'll get it next time."

THE WEEKS ALL BLEND TOGETHER AND IT'S FINALLY THE LAST WEEK.

"OK, which way are we trying to score?"

Silence. (An accurate answer, but not what I want to hear.)

"We are kicking at that goal! If you see the ball, run to it and kick it to that goal, OK?"

A few kids nod heads! (SUCCESS!)

They go on the field and the yelling continues.

A young player gets the ball in the open and heads to the goal.

"KICK IT IN!!!"

My young star is about to score when he finally hears me yell and he stops, turns to me and says, "What?"

Obviously, ignoring coaches is something my team needs a little work on. But I think that next year we could be great ... if I just knew what this clipboard was for ...

125

SPIKE-FREE ZONE

I knew this conversation was coming.

I've been preparing my responses for years, so I would say just the right thing and not confuse or upset my son.

What I didn't expect was that the conversation would come so soon and that I would be so nervous about it.

Of course, I'm talking about my son's hair.

This topic causes me fits for a number of reasons, all of which are rooted (no pun intended) in my own hair and the often loud and ridiculous arguments I had with my dad when I was growing up.

When I was growing up, my dad was generally a pretty cool guy. More than a few times, he calmed my mom down when I came home late or did something stupid.

He let me listen to the music I wanted to listen to and generally let me wear the clothes I wanted to wear.

But when it came to hair, my dad was Stalin.

"As long as you live under my roof, you will not go around looking like some hippie," he said to me.

I wanted long hair. I don't mean just a bit shaggy. I wanted dangle-to-the butt, scrapin'-on-the-ground long. Of course, in my teenage mind, the only thing keeping me from having sex 24 hours a day was a dad who wouldn't let me grow my hair out so I could look like all those guys in the music videos who got all the girls.

I could not understand why my dad was so hung up on my hair — and I was pretty ticked off about it.

The minute I graduated from high school, I vowed to never visit a barbershop again.

And I didn't ... due to my vow and the fact I had to choose between a haircut and buying beer.

Through four years in college, my hair grew (although I never looked like those cool guys on MTV — not sure how I messed that part up).

After graduating from high school, I soon realized that most prospective employers were run by guys like my dad who didn't really care for my choice in hairstyle, so I chopped it all off. It was a horrible time in my life.

It was then that I took another vow: I would never be so authoritarian to my son as to dictate his hairstyle. It was a sacred vow. In fact, when my wife and I first talked about having kids, I told her that the only thing I cared about was that we let the kid pick his own hairstyle.

Then, my 4-year-old says, on the way to the barbershop, "I want spikes."

"Huh?"

"I want spikes. I want my hair to stick up like that kid on TV."

I didn't know what kid he was talking about, but I didn't really care. My kid was NOT going to have spiked hair!

"No," I said, breaking my vow.

"Why?"

I wanted to say, "Because you'd look like an idiot and quite honestly I would hate it." But I figured that would only make him want it more.

I tried to explain that he wasn't old enough to make such a decision — just like he wasn't old enough to drive a car.

My logic must have worked, because he completely ignored it and said, "I WANT SPIKES."

At this point, I was left with only one option and it ended the conversation:

"As long as you are living under my roof..."

BIRTHDAY PARTY STRATEGIC PLANNING

My son's birthday parties used to be so easy.

We would have a simple get-together with our family, Grandma and one or two of my son's friends.

Now, by "friend" I mean, of course, "the child of a friend of my wife and I."

Until now, we were basically able to tell my son who his friends were.

Two things happened to change that:

First, he was turning five years old, which was apparently the year that he became aware of this whole "friend-scam" thing.

Second, my wife planned the party while I was out of town.

Instead of the traditional party planning we had done (i.e. We picked a time and date that worked for us and invited our friends and their kids), my wife took a whole new route. She asked my son what he wanted.

"Who are the friends you'd like at your party?"

She was expecting him to rattle off a few names for her guest list. But not only did my son get wise to his parents' scam, he also invented his own.

Now, don't get me wrong. My son is very friendly and I'm sure that he truly enjoys the company of all 17 kids he listed off to my wife, but I couldn't help thinking that he was working out the first math problem all kids discover: the larger the number of kids equals a larger number of presents.

When I called my wife from out of town, she informed me that we now had 41 people (with the parents) planning to attend. This was a larger crowd than at his previous four birthday parties combined!

That many people would not have been a major problem if we had stuck to standard birthday party etiquette: kids come, kids play, kids sing and eat cake and then the birthday kid opens his presents and sends everyone home with a party bag full of cheap toys that break 30 seconds later.

This is tradition and there's good reason for it: It's cheap and it's fast.

But that didn't work for this party and things got plenty more complicated because of two people: my wife and my mom.

My wife decided that if we were going to have that many people at the time we had planned (based on the party room she booked), we were also going to have to serve dinner.

This now added extra time to the party, which meant booking more time in the place.

When you get a bunch of kids in one place, load them up with sugar and only one kid gets all the presents, the last thing anyone wants is for it to be longer.

My wife also was against the whole "cheap party bag" thing. Why she wanted to buck generations of tradition on this, I'll never understand. Instead, we bought these little flashing safety lights for all the kids and she insisted that I install the batteries for each one for the party so the kids could play with them.

So, I spent several hours unscrewing the battery panel (why do kids' toys have screw-on battery panels these days?) and making sure each one worked properly. All of this was exhausting, but then my mom got involved. Actually, she was in California, but her influence reached across the distance and created havoc. You see, my mom instilled in me some bizarre trait that makes it physically impossible to buy a birthday cake for my kids. It must be homemade — and, for some reason, it pretty much has to be complicated.

So, the night before the big event, I stayed up late icing my son's cake with newly arthritic hands. And since our party list length now rivaled the passenger list of the Titanic, I also had to ice 48 cupcakes.

In the end, my son was thrilled, all the kids had a pretty good time, the parents were not too unhappy about the change in birthday party protocol, and we had plenty of cupcakes to take home.

But next year, I am planning the party.

AIN'T THEY CLEVER

CAREER COUNSELING

Like most parents, I can't help but imagine what my kids will do for a living when they are older.

We parents watch our kids and we pick out those subtle nuances that hint at a career in some high profile (and hopefully high-paying) career.

When a kid throws a toy at the head of another child across the room, parents (OK, maybe I just mean dads) have two thoughts that go through their heads: "That was dangerous; I should punish my child now" AND "Dang, that was a good throw and he's left handed; heck we could get a $10 million signing bonus!"

Please don't take this as my attempt to "pigeonhole" my kids. I am simply observing their natural behavior and figuring out a way I can eventually retire really, really, really young.

Here are a few of my sons' career options and a few examples of why they would be great at it:

POLITICIAN

Skill: Problem solving.

Incident: My oldest son was at day care and spotted a large mud-puddle.

Puddles are a natural draw to boys. They are like that bubble-wrap boys have to pop and the hoops boys have to shoot through.

Boys must jump in mud-puddles. When we grow up, boys become men. And we men don't have to jump in puddles. But if we are driving in a car, we will cross three lanes of traffic to drive fast through a puddle just to see the spray.

Anyway, boys like puddles and my son has an obsession. But he knows that when he jumps in a puddle, he and his clothing will get wet.

So, my son sees a problem: There is a mud-puddle I could jump into, but my clothes will get messed up.

And he tries to find a solution: Mom put extra clothes in my backpack, so I can go ahead and jump.

Then he sees another problem: I don't have an extra pair of shoes.

And another solution: If I take my shoes off, I can jump in with my socks and I'll be fine.

That was the explanation he gave when I asked why he was wearing all new clothes and yet his shoes were perfectly clean. Bill Clinton would have given an intern to be able to think like that on his feet (with or without shoes)!

LAWYER
Skills: Finding loopholes
Incident: A different day and a different mud-puddle.

This one took place as my wife was picking the boys up from daycare. They were going out to the car and my oldest spotted the puddle.

He knew he was headed home where he had some dry shoes, so he decided to go banzai into the puddle. Before my wife could catch him, he was crawling around on all fours in the puddle.

Of course, my wife was mad, but she couldn't really do anything about the fact he was covered in mud. So, she tossed him in his car seat next to his brother.

When little brother started crying, Mom handed him a cookie. Well, my oldest is a cookie freak so he asked for one.

"Your hands are all dirty from the mud. You can't have a cookie with muddy hands," my wife said, thinking that was at least some punishment for his mud bath.

When she finally pulled into the garage at home, she reached back to unhook the boys and she noticed my oldest's hands were perfectly clean.

He said, "Now can I have a cookie?"

"How did you ... " she started to ask when he smiled and she saw his muddy face. Yes, my son decided that if he couldn't eat a cookie with dirty hands, he would clean them off himself ... by licking all the mud off!

Doesn't that sound like every lawyer you ever met?

CELEBRITY IMPERSONATOR
Skill: Entertaining crowds by mimicking other folks.

Incident: My youngest is just learning about animals and the sounds they make. He loves to say, "Baa" and "Moo" and "Quack" for no apparent reason.

But when you ask him what sound an animal makes, the answer is always the same...

"What does a lion say?"

"ROAAAARR!!"

"What does a sheep say?"

"ROAAAARR!!"

"What does that annoying woman on 'The Weakest Link' say?"

"ROAAAARR!!"

Well, two out of three isn't bad.

THE TRICK'S ON ME

There's the guy who can tie a cherry stem with his tongue.

There's the one who can recite every joke ever told to him and has the whole bar laughing.

There's the guy who can take a dollar bill, a paper clip and a matchbook and create a perfect-to-scale model of the Eiffel Tower.

That's not me.

I don't have any of those skills — those skills that seem to come in handy during boring parties or for attempting to liven up a bar.

I did try to learn these skills. But there is nothing more pathetic than someone who tries a party trick and fails. The closest I ever got was being able to name all nine planets in order — but, oddly, that doesn't really impress anyone. Eventually, I gave up.

When my sons were born, I realized I now had the props for some of the best party tricks ever. I figured all I had to do was teach my sons some silly task or have them memorize something odd and I was on my way to being king of the party tricks.

It started when I was reading my oldest son a book about Curious George and his visit to Mount Rushmore. My son kept asking me about the names of the people in the mountain. So, I told him — over and over again.

Little kids are like sponges — they soak up everything (and they are usually wet and slimy, but that's another issue). Anyway, my son remembered those names and we would amaze our friends at parties when my 2-year-old son would rattle off the names of the presidents.

The highlight was when my son was in daycare. The teacher told me that another child was talking about a recent trip to the Black Hills and seeing Mount Rushmore. She said my son stood up and said, "George Washington, Abraham Lincoln, Thomas Jefferson and Teddy Roosevelt."

The teacher added, "I was stunned. I didn't know what to say because I wasn't even sure if he was right."

But soon the rush of Rushmore became less and less exciting. We needed something new to dazzle the crowds.

Finally, it came to me. I taught my son how to write his name. He turned out to be great at it. At not-quite-3-years-old, he became an expert in writing his name.

Everyone commented on how good he was. He practiced all the time. He wrote his name in the steam on a mirror, on pieces of paper and on many of his toys.

My son loves to write his name. And it finally came back to hurt me the other day.

My wife was picking up the kids. She took them out to the van and started talking to a friend. She latched my youngest in his seat and then went looking for the oldest.

She found him around the front of the van. He had found an old rusty nail in the parking lot and had etched his name (with perfect form, I might add) across the hood of the van.

"Mom, look what I did!" he said as he smiled proudly and waited for his praise.

My wife was dumbfounded.

When I saw it, I knew that it was at least a little bit my fault.

My wife gets frequent comments about the new front-end design of her van, including someone the other day that said, after hearing the story, "I can't believe he can do that at 3-years-old."

I guess the front of our van is a small price to pay for that kind of glory.

DAYS OF WHINE AND "NO"SES

Every child comes into this world with a certain set of skills. Each of these skills has a place in the world he or she will live in.

For instance, the cry. Crying is an amazingly effective way to get a parent's attention when the kid is in trouble ... or when the kid wants to drive the parent nuts.

The big eyes and adorable smile of a child also serve a purpose. They are the reason parents don't get truly irked by all the crying.

Kids have others skills (pooping, peeing, eating, and burping) that all have a rather obvious function and purpose for existing.

The problem I have been having lately is determining the exact reason for and origin of the most amazing skill all kids have: the whine.

Whining is universal. It's done for the same reasons and in the same tone in every country in the world (I know this because, well, I just made it up, but it sounds true, so just go with it).

To truly understand the whine, you have to know all the subtle nuances of it.

A whine is not a cry — although the child tries to make it sound like it. In the early stages of a whine, the vowels of each word will get drawn out. As the request is denied or ignored, the vowels become longer and can begin to sound like sentences of their own.

An experienced whiner will try to avoid sounding like a whiner by emphasizing a different word in the request so it sounds like a logical argument.

"Dad, I WAAAAAANT to have the bluuuuuue cup!"

"No, that's your brother's cup."

"But, I waaaaant to have the BLUUUUUUEE cup!"

There are also different types of whines that serve slightly different purposes.

First, there's the "grass is always greener" whine. This comes when a child chooses one thing and then promptly wants what the other child chose.

Second, there's the "I want" whine. This can most often be heard in the toy aisles of major department stores. "But, Mom, I WAAAAANT to have a RAAAACE CAAAAR!"

The all-time greatest whine, however, is the totally irrational, unexplainable whine. This one comes from nowhere, means nothing, but still drives the parent crazy.

"Billy is loooooking at me again."

"I don't waaant to drive thiiiis waaaaay home."

Every kid does it. I am still trying to figure out why. I mean, I know it doesn't work. Usually it's only a prime indicator that the kid needs a nap, because the whine-to-success ratio can't be good enough to warrant all that energy.

When my kids start whining, I barely pay attention. My reasoning is that if they see they don't get anything out of it, they'll stop it.

But they don't.

I hear it at night when they don't want to go to bed. I hear it when we pass up the Choco-covered-donut-flavored-cookie-shaped cereal with the fancy prize inside.

I hear it when one of my sons gets the first bowl of oatmeal in the morning when the other one wanted it (followed quickly by the other one whining that he didn't get the Scooby-Doo bowl).

The whining continues. It's been four years now and I see no sign of it stopping.

Maybe my kids know something I don't. Maybe whining works on other people. Maybe I've been an idiot all these years because I don't whine more.

"But Boss, I REALLY REALLY WAAAAANT a raise!"

"Honey, I don't WAAAANT to go out dancing!"

Hmm, maybe they're on to something. This requires a little more research.

And a lot more vowels.

NO MORE DIAPER DOO-DEE

I can finally see some light at the end of the tunnel ... it's been a LONG tunnel ... it's been a LONG and SMELLY tunnel ...

But there is light (and hopefully fresh air) ahead.

It has been more than five years since my wife and I entered the parental adventure of dealing with diapers. We have now hosted two kids through this passage of life and I couldn't be happier to be done with it.

By my calculations, my sons have forced us to change more than 10,000 diapers over the last five years — and I personally have changed at least three of them.

My youngest son has recently decided to try using the potty. The important part of that sentence is "try." As any parent of a boy knows, even the word "using" only means he's pointing in the general direction of the potty. When a boy is "trying" to "use" the potty that means you are usually left with a clean up that requires sandblasting equipment.

However, I know that "trying" eventually leads to "using" regularly which leads to me not having to change diapers and — even better — not having to buy more.

There are advantages to diapers, of course.

Imagine this scene: You are in a huge open field surrounded by thousands of other families with kids all carrying baskets hoping to hunt down a few Easter eggs. As the countdown begins to the mad rush, your youngest looks at you with the terror that only little kids (and parents) have and says, "I HAVE TO PEE!"

As a parent, a mental stopwatch begins in your head. You know that you now have about 15 seconds to find this child a bathroom. That's when diapers come in handy. It is so much easier to just say, "OK, go ahead" and he'd be done before the egg countdown got to three.

Instead you make a mad rush through (and sometimes over) a sea of people to save the day (and your son's pants). And end up missing the entire Easter egg hunt.

So, it's not that diapers are all bad. It's just that there is the complete headache that goes along with them. There is no other piece of clothing that requires a "bag" that comes with it. The diaper bag has been a constant companion for my wife and me for the past five years.

The diaper bag contains all the tools of the trade plus extra changes of clothes, snacks, toys, markers and paper and, I believe, a copy of the Magna Carta (just in case).

And we are about to get rid of the diaper bag.

We can also say goodbye to those hours of playing the wonderful game, "Did he or didn't he?" This game usually takes place in a car, but it is also available in the non-travel version at someone else's home or at some event where it would be a little unseemly to pull out the back of my son's pants to see if he did a No. 2.

"Did he or didn't he?"

"I don't know," I say as we begin minute 10 of an hour-long drive. "I think that's just the feedlots you're smelling."

"I'm not sure. Maybe he did. We should probably pull over."

So, we do. And he didn't, so we drive some more.

"I think he definitely did this time..."

I will be very sad to see that game go away. (Not!) Of course it will be replaced with the, "I know I didn't have to go before we left, but I've been in the car for a whole 10 seconds so you HAVE to find a potty NOW!" game.

Veteran parents always laugh when I tell them how happy I am that I'm almost done with diapers. They say, "That's nothing. Just wait until they start..." and they end the sentence with some horribly disgusting thing their child did.

But after five years of being in this tunnel, I'm looking forward to just about any other scenery.

BRIBERY:
A FISH STORY

Parenting survives on bribes. It's just that simple.

Oh sure, those psychology folks will tell you it's "positive reinforcement" or "reward" or "candy," but let's face it, it all comes down to bribery.

This is a system that has gone on since the dawn of time. And it generally works well. Parents promise a bribe to get desired behavior. Kid does desired behavior. Parent gives bribe. Everyone is happy.

The only real glitch in the system is when the parent doesn't give a whole lot of thought to the bribe. Recently, to save my sanity and save on doing laundry every night, my wife and I asked my son what he would like if he could keep his bed pee-free for seven days.

He must have just watched some ocean show because he said, "I want a fish."

Parents do a quick calculation when these deals are in the works: cost of item vs. benefit of behavior. To our later dismay, our minds told us it was well worth the 98 cents for a fish to not have to deal with yet another "Oops MOMMY!"

Plus, I figured they could learn some valuable life lessons from fish included feeding, caring and, eventually, flushing! My concern with getting fish, of course, was the fear over the one question every kid eventually asks: "Dad, where do fish sticks come from?"

Despite that fear, my wife and I agreed. And my son, to our amazement, fulfilled his end of the bargain.

Because it would be cruel to let one kid have a new pet and not the other, we were now obligated to get two fish. I still thought we were getting off cheap. I mean in all those old cartoons, they show goldfish swimming happily in a little bowl.

When we went to the pet store and picked out our fishbowls, the guy who was about to scoop up the fish my sons wanted said, "You're not going to put these fish in THOSE bowls are you?"

He said it with a tone that suggested, "Are you stark-raving nuts?"

So, I said, "Yes."

"Why would you do that?"

"Well, it says right on the side of the bowl that this is a goldfish bowl and those are goldfish. I'm no pet store employee, but that seems to make sense to me."

"Read that," he said, as he pointed to a laminated article on the wall. The article pointed out the tragedy that has befallen generations of goldfish: the mistaken belief that goldfish are happy in bowls, when in fact they are tortured by a certain lack of oxygen. It was like "Roots" with gills.

"So, what are we supposed to get?"

"Well, those tanks are very nice," he said pointing toward a commission-stuffing megalotank that included, I think, tiny massage jets for when the fish get sore from swimming all the time.

My sons were not really paying attention, fortunately, because they were too busy trying to keep track of the exact fish they wanted from the tank of 734.

We ended up with a low-end model with a pump and plenty of goodies to put in the tank for the fish to play with.

The two fish that came home with us were soon a part of the family — Henry and Skeletor Fish.

We followed all of the instructions and soon Henry and Skeletor were swimming happily around the tank in my sons' room. My sons were so excited to sit there and watch them ... for about 10 seconds.

"What else can they do?" my youngest asked.

Despite an overwhelming lack of interest, the fish stayed with our kids through the night. And the tank bubbled ... and the water rolled and splashed a bit ...

And by the time morning rolled around, both of my sons had peed in their beds.

So much for bribery.

MY SON AS HEN-NY YOUNGMAN

Most people think they are ... but they're not. This statement could relate to many things (good looking, rich, smart, good drivers, etc.), but I'm talking about being funny.

I think the case could be made for the phrase "I'm funny" as being one of the biggest misconceptions people have about themselves (heck, some people have this false perception so strongly they force it upon others in a newspaper column!).

Why do we want to be funny? Well, when people lie about the things they are "really" attracted to in another person, the phrase "a good sense of humor" always comes up.

I figure if it's important enough for people to lie about, I better make sure my sons have that skill when they get out in the real world. But how do you develop a sense of humor or teach someone to be funny?

When I was a kid, the key was having a receptive audience. I'm not talking about parents here. A good audience will laugh at the same joke 400 times in a row. Parents stop giggling after replay No. 12.

For me, my audience was my younger sister. When we were young, I could make her laugh with minimal effort and do it repeatedly. Perhaps my greatest humor achievement was a short song I developed that went like this "I don't care / I don't care / So, just poop in your underwear."

My sister would giggle so hard she couldn't breathe when I sang my little ditty. That song was comic gold for a kid because all you really have to do to make a kid laugh is insert the words: poop, underwear, booger, pee, butt, nose or toots.

The comedian George Carlin has his "Seven Dirty Words" for adults, but these are the ones that send kids into hysterics.

My sons have learned this lesson with no help from me. You see they each have a very willing audience in each other. The hard part is they both think they are the funny one and so they both try to top each other's jokes all the time.

And beyond the seven words kids like, my sons have found another: chicken. For some reason this word sets both of them off whether it is used alone or in conjunction with any of the other words.

"Daddy, guess where I want to go? CHICKEN!"

"I want to wear Chicken boogers to school."

It doesn't matter that my wife and I don't think this is funny, because whichever son says it, I know the other son is going to laugh so hard that it makes up for our sour faces.

What is really strange is that there are times when we want to get our sons to laugh and so we will try to use one of their "classic" jokes to put them in a good mood. But when Mom or Dad says "chicken" it's just not funny. In fact, we have to really sell it to even get a giggle for a word like "toots."

I got to thinking that maybe the reason so many people think they are funny when they aren't is because they were able to make their siblings laugh when they were young. This got me a little worried about my boys.

I mean if they went out in the real world with their current material, they would get crushed. I pictured my son sitting in a boardroom at a meeting and tossing out the phrase "chicken poop" as if it were the funniest thing ever.

So, I tried some comic training with my sons. I tried to teach them some "classic" jokes to broaden their repertoire.

Of course, this was a miserable failure. This is how their jokes came out...

"Knock. Knock"

"Who's there?"

"CHICKEN!"

(This was a house favorite for about 14 days straight.)

As was this:

"Why did the chicken cross the road?"

"To go POOP!"

Then, one day it happened. My son thought up a joke on his own and it wasn't bad. "What do you get when you cross a monster and a president? ... Lincoln-Stein!"

This got a real laugh from both my wife and me. And we kept laughing after he told it to us seven or eight more times. When the laughs died down though, he reverted to his safety zone and the joke soon ended with "Lincoln-Chicken!"

My other son likes that one even more.

I guess the important thing isn't that they are funny, but that they think they are ... CHICKEN.

A STICKY SITUATION

I try to prepare myself for anything. I am a parent. I must be ready to roll with any punch and ride any wave.

And then, my wife tells me about my son's day.

"He inhaled a sticker today."

"What?"

"He inhaled a sticker."

My son is only 6, but my first thought was, "Is this some strange new drug? And how did my 6-year-old get hold of it? Why didn't they cover this on ER?"

My drug fear faded (that will be an ill-prepared moment in the future!). For now, I had to deal with the current issue.

You need to be prepared to deal with strange stuff as a parent. But inhaling stickers just went a little beyond my personal bizarre scope.

"How did that happen?"

"Ask him."

My son was looking up at me with a big smile on his face.

"What happened?"

"Well, I was in school and we had these little happy face stickers and I put one on my nose to cover up my nose hole."

"Why?"

I knew it was a dumb question when I asked, but I was interested in his thought process.

"I just wanted to."

"OK, so then what happened?"

"I don't know how but my finger just pushed it up into my nose."

"Your finger did it? But you didn't do it?"

"Yeah."

"So, then what happened?"

"They took me to the office and shined a flashlight up my nose, but they couldn't find it."

My wife was hiding her head to try not to show she was laughing.

Parents generally have three choices in responding to a child: Laughing, compassion or sternness. My wife covered the laughing angle, so I knew I should either be worried about him regarding this foreign smiley sticker floating around in his tiny lungs or I should be stern and explain why sticking a sticker up your nose is not a very smart idea.

Neither one quite worked. I was completely ill prepared as a parent to deal with that situation.

My sister-in-law happened to be visiting us that night. We started talking about where the inhaled smiley may have gone.

She then remembered a college course where the professor, in a completely dark room, shined a bright light in her mouth to show the class her sinuses were lit up. I didn't ask what class this was, but I assumed it had something to do with tax preparation.

So, my sister-in-law had an idea that we could shine a light in my son's mouth and see if the sticker was now decorating the walls of his sinuses.

Of course I didn't believe this would actually work and I accused her of having a little too much fun at college and hallucinating the whole thing.

This got her riled up and she went searching through our house for a flashlight. Anyone who has kids knows that you may have 59 different flashlights in the house but none of them will have batteries that work. The only thing she could find was a small, toy flashlight that only lit up as long as you held the button down.

The family gathered around for our post-dinner entertainment as my sister-in-law shoved the tiny flashlight into her mouth plus one hand to hold it and another to hold the button down.

The trick did work but we decided against trying a similar attack on my son. As for my son's sticker, we're just hoping that's the largest thing he tries to shove up his nose — but I bet it's not.

The real problem came when my son was watching his aunt and her flashlight trick.

My son piped up soon. "Dad, can I do that when she's done?"

My parenting response was quick with a standard answer. "No, we don't put toys in our mouths."

"But she's doing it."

"Well, she's trying to show us something."

"I want to show you something, too!"

For the second time in less than an hour, I was completely at a loss as a parent.

I suppose I better get used to it.

THE FIRST DAY

I don't remember my first day of kindergarten. I was probably a little too obsessed with the concept of recess and snack time for it to really register in my memory.

So, the closest thing I can compare my oldest son's first day at kindergarten to is the day my parents dropped me off at college.

I remember that day. Heck, I had dreamed of that day from the first time my dad told me to take out the garbage.

I remember loading all of my worldly possessions into milk crates and stuffing them into my new dorm room. I remember my dad checking the place out, looking around for something to fix — something that he could use his male-emotional coping skills on. When guys have to deal with emotions in my family, it usually means something is going to be constructed with power tools.

My mom was a different story. She kept saying things like, "My little boy has grown up" and tears welled up in her eyes. She promised me she wouldn't cry, because it probably would have killed me socially in my new "cool" place.

"OK, bye," I said with an implied emphasis on "Bye."

She gave me a hug — a little longer than I wanted, probably too short for her. I found out years later that she went back to the car with my dad and cried the whole way back home.

I just didn't understand. I mean I was so darn glad to be free.

Now, I get it.

I got it as I stood in a brightly colored room with letters and numbers on the wall as other parents got the same message as their children went to their first day of "big kid school."

For days leading up to the event, my wife and I told our son about how he was going to love his new school and that he was a big boy now and that we were so proud of him.

We didn't think he was listening.

The night before the big day, he admitted that he was scared. He said he was nervous about the school and that he wanted his mommy and daddy to stay with him at school all day. I tried to explain that we couldn't do that and he would really love the school and all the other lies parents tell kids to get them to go to sleep.

That night I thought about all the other "first days" I have seen. I worked for newspapers for 10 years — so that's about 10 years of having an editor tell me, "Go cover the first day of kindergarten." It was the same story every year. The photographer would find the kid having the hardest time saying goodbye to mom and he would shoot an adorable crying picture. My job was to interview the parents (who were also usually crying). They always said the same thing: "I can't believe he's going to school already." "It seems like just yesterday we brought him home from the hospital." "He's such a big boy now."

They all read the same, but people loved to read them.

Now, all I thought about was my son being the front-page-picture child for the newspaper as he cried his eyes out while being ripped from the safety of his parents and forced into the "cruel" world of institutional education.

On the morning of the big event, I think I was more nervous than my son was. I just wanted him to be happy. Just get through the next 20 minutes without tears.

We got to school early so he could get used to the environment. My wife snapped pictures and I tried to explain to him what all the places in the building were for (cafeteria, gym, classrooms).

Finally, the door opened and the kids were able to flood into the room. For the first day, the school allows parents to come into the room to drop their kid off — either they are kind, understanding people or they just want to make it possible for the newspaper to get good shots of kids crying.

My son found his name on the wall and hung up his bag. The teacher then asked the parents to pin nametags on their kids. My son would have none of that. He wanted to do it. He was a big boy after all.

As the rest of the parents and kids came into the room, my son found a seat at a table.

This was the moment I had feared.

We had to say goodbye. This was when the hissy-fit would come. This was when we would have to uncurl his vise-like grip from our legs so we could leave the room.

Except it didn't happen.

"We're going to leave now."

"OK, Bye," he said as he turned to talk to other kids and draw.

That was it. No tears. Nothing.

That's when I knew the feeling my mom had back in my dorm room. I also understood why those parents I interviewed over the years all said the same thing.

It all happens so quickly.